HOLD UP HER HANDS!

HOLD UP HER HANDS!

Questions, Answers, and A Message to Preaching Women, and Those Who Oppose Them

David Scott, Ed.D., D.Min.

PCB

Published by Purple Chair Books and Educational Products, LLC

First Printing, 2025

Copyright © David Scott, 2025

Scott, David 1969-

Hold Up Her Hands!

By David Scott

ISBN: 978-1-953671-04-2

Subject: Christian Life/ Spiritual

Printed in the United States of America

Interior designed by Md Al Amin

Cover designed by Sadia A@Sadia_coverz

All rights reserved. No part of this publication may be reproduced, stored in a retrieval system, or transmitted in any form or by any means- electronic, photocopy, or recording- without the publisher's prior written permission. The only exception is brief quotations in printed reviews.

DEDICATION

I dedicate this book to all the brave, talented, gifted, and anointed women called and chosen to preach the Word of God. It is also in memory of my beloved big sister in Christ, Pastor Terri Michelle Givens, a genuinely gifted, powerful, and spirit-filled vessel and ambassador of Christ Jesus.

ACKNOWLEDGMENT

I want to thank my beautiful, faithful companion and treasure in this life, First Lady Tamara Scott, a.k.a. The Boss. Because of your endless prayers, support, and encouragement, I continue reaching for deeper places and higher plateaus in our Savior. Thank you for all you do and for encouraging me to be my best for Christ.

TABLE OF CONTENTS

PREFACE 1
INTRODUCTION 4
1. WOMEN AS LEADERS 10
2. PERMITTED SERVICE 19
3. MEN AND WOMEN MUST PREACH! 28
4. WHY DO WOMEN PREACH? 37
5. THE CALL TO PREACH 44
6. WORK OF THE HOLY SPIRIT 52
7. WHAT DID PAUL (REALLY) SAY? 58
8. WHAT DID JESUS SAY? 68
9. WHAT DID JESUS DO? 76
10. JEREMIAH'S DECLARATION 83
11. FAITHFUL LABORERS 89
12. JOEL'S PROPHESY 95
TO THE ELECT WOMEN IN CHRIST 105
TO MALE LEADERS 108
FINAL THOUGHTS AND A PRAYER 112
MY PRAYER 114
WOMEN MINISTRY LEADER FIRSTS 115

PREFACE

For too long, women in the Church have been made to feel that their worth and contributions are secondary to those of their male counterparts. This attitude does not align with how Jesus viewed women. On the contrary, He valued, loved, protected, and affirmed them at every opportunity. Jesus cared deeply for all His followers and servants, especially the so-called "weaker vessels." Much of His earthly ministry was focused on uplifting women and liberating them from the biased and second-class treatment prevalent in His time's society.

The fourth chapter of the Book of John provides a significant example of Jesus' attitude toward women. In this scenario, Jesus breaks away from societal and traditional norms. He engages in an extensive conversation with a Samaritan woman, which is notably unusual. After discussing the life-giving water He could offer, Jesus tells her, "The time is coming, and has now arrived, when true worshippers will worship the Father in spirit and truth, for the Father is seeking those who will worship Him."

After meeting Jesus, the woman forgot why she had come to the well. She left her water jar behind and returned to the city, telling the men, "Come, see a man... could this be the Christ?" Her encounter with a man who looked beyond customs, practices, social norms, and cultural traditions gave her validation, dignity, and a sense of value and humanity. As a result, she was forever changed and felt compelled to share her experience with others.

It is ridiculous to conclude that God places a more significant or higher value on one gender over the other. This concept is a human invention, an idea far from God. God has no favorites and shows no partiality. Women are of equal value as their male counterparts. Undeniably, women are equally dedicated, reliable, capable, and committed to the work of the ministry as male ministers. Statistically, women make up over 60% of the Protestant Christian church, but over 87% of pastors are male. Why would God limit the work and function of any of his servants merely based on gender? That is not the mind of God. On the contrary, it is more plausible that it results from the desire, work, and manipulation of egotistical and insecure men.

God does not regard gender when choosing whom to use. He selects individuals based solely on their willingness and availability, regardless of whether they are male or female. Any accomplishments for the kingdom of God, achieved by either gender, are through the work and power of the Holy Spirit. When God pours out His Spirit on both men and women, it is the same Spirit and power at work.

The power that rests upon women in ministry today is a fulfillment of God's promise and word. Who can deny the hand and movement of God? Why do men resist when God himself said it would be? We can neither refute nor deny the words of the prophet Joel recorded in Acts 2:17, *"And it shall come to pass in the last days, saith God, I will pour out of my spirit upon all flesh: and your sons and your daughters shall prophesy."*

This book aims to empower women preachers, teachers, pastors, and evangelists to affirm their calling confidently. It aims to inspire women to boldly proclaim the word of God, just as Paul instructed Timothy. I challenge and encourage you to preach without compromise. Preach with all your heart. Speak without apology. Share your message as you were called to, regardless of any adversity, opposition, need, or lack you may encounter. If God has indeed chosen and called you to preach, do so unashamedly, sharing God's unfailing and powerful word with the anointing and strength He provides. Prove your calling and election through the fulfillment of your ministry. Trust in God!

In John 9:37, Jesus says, "The harvest is plentiful, but the laborers are few. Therefore, pray that the Lord of the harvest will send laborers into His vineyard." As His laborers, we are called to work—preaching, teaching, exhorting, compelling, and winning souls for the Kingdom of God. Those called to serve the Lord are accountable not to any mortal man but to God alone. If the Father of Lights has called us, we must respond. We owe a debt to our living Savior, Christ Jesus. Let no one look down upon your calling. Remember the words of Proverbs 11:30: "He who wins souls is wise."

To all the brave and courageous women who choose to obey and follow Christ, I encourage you as faithful ministers and laborers for the Master. As the Apostle Paul said to Timothy, I say to you: "I charge you, therefore, before God and the Lord Jesus Christ, who will judge the living and the dead at His appearing and His kingdom: Preach the word; be ready in season and out of season; reprove, rebuke, and exhort with all patience and teaching. The time will come when people will not accept sound doctrine but will gather teachers who satisfy their desires, having itching ears. They will turn away from the truth and embrace myths. But you, be watchful in all things, endure afflictions, do the work of an evangelist, and fulfill your ministry."

INTRODUCTION

Women continue to make remarkable advancements across nearly all industries and spheres of life. In every area where they have been given the opportunity, women have consistently demonstrated their ability to perform and excel beyond expectations. They have repeatedly shown that they are more than capable and ready to meet any challenge when given access and equal opportunities.

Despite demonstrating their remarkable abilities, skills, talents, and resilience, women have faced obstacles from those who, with equal determination, seek to hinder their opportunities simply because of their gender. Nevertheless, women worldwide continue to showcase the absurdity of such opposition by excelling and often outperforming their male counterparts.

Few industries worldwide completely exclude women or deny them access. Women have demonstrated their capability as strong, competent, and effective leaders. They hold senior and executive leadership roles in nearly every country. However, there remains one significant area where women face denial and opposition without logical justification: the church.

The New and Old Testament scriptures prove female leadership in the early church. However, some men work tirelessly to prevent women from assuming pastoral roles. This resistance stems from a refusal to engage in logical reasoning, as they cling to their beliefs despite the

Biblical assertion that God created both men and women as equals. Genesis 1:27 states, "So God created human beings in his image. He created them in God's image; male and female, he created them." God loves and values both genders equally, as both Adam and Eve are made in the image of God.

As we examine scripture, we find no specific passage that forbids or denies the ordination or consecration of women to the pastoral office. God does not show favoritism. Unlike humans, God does not emphasize the gender of those who serve Him. God demonstrates an absence of bias. When we explore the scriptures with an open heart, mind, and a commitment to unbiased scholarship, it becomes clear that any perceived distinctions between men and women dissolve through baptism in the Lord Jesus Christ. This is affirmed in Galatians 3:27-28, which states, "All who have been united with Christ in baptism have put on Christ, like putting on new clothes. There is no longer Jew or Gentile, slave or free, male and female. For you are all one in Christ Jesus."

The belief held by some that women are denied, excluded, or forbidden from serving Christ in any capacity—including the pastoral office or the bishopric—is unfounded, as it is not supported by Scripture or by Christ himself. When we examine Christ's actions and attitudes toward women, it becomes clear that Jesus trained, cultivated, and developed many loyal and faithful women in His ministry. Additionally, it is undeniable that Christ deliberately chose two faithful, capable, and trustworthy women to be the first evangelists and preachers tasked with proclaiming the gospel to men.

If those in opposition were sincere and open to truth and reason, it would be entirely plausible to argue that the Apostle Paul's letters addressed specific concerns and issues related to particular churches rather than serving as a universal manifesto intended for all times and all churches. To believe otherwise is highly improbable, irrational, and unfounded.

The words attributed to the Apostle Paul that are often used to restrict women and prevent them from holding senior leadership positions are frequently misinterpreted and taken out of context. When analyzing Paul's teachings, it is essential to consider the cultural context in which they were written. We must remember that more than 2,100 years have passed since Paul's time; he could not have possibly anticipated the societal changes, customs, practices, personal freedoms, and advancements in gender equality that would develop over the centuries. Many of the instructions he provided were explicitly intended for a unique cultural setting and should be understood as such.

Christ is the Lord of all, and He chooses whomever He wills. God shows no partiality or favoritism toward men or women. The Holy Spirit is available to everyone and is freely given to both men and women. God seeks those who are willing and available to serve. He grants gifts to all, regardless of gender, to build His church. The scripture is clear on this matter. Ephesians 4:11-13 states: "These are the gifts Christ gave to the church: the apostles, the prophets, the evangelists, and the pastors and teachers. Their responsibility is to equip God's people to do His work and build up the church, the body of Christ. This will continue until we all attain such unity in our faith and knowledge of God's Son that we will mature in the Lord, measuring up to the full standard of Christ."

God gives both males and females gifts, which should not be impeded, stifled, or hindered. Regardless of the beliefs and ideas of some, God acts according to His own will. He does not require anyone to restrain His male or female servants. When God bestows gifts, He intends for them to be used to achieve His purposes. The Lord desires that all be saved and none perish. However, as each day passes, the world grows increasingly dark. Our testimony is vital; the light of Christ must be brought into this dark world to effect change. The sheep need faithful shepherds; unlike foolish humans, God is not concerned with gender.

No matter the plans, determination, or efforts of those who oppose, God will continue to raise and use both men and women as leaders in His church. The mission to which God has called us is far too important, vital, and eternally significant to exclude anointed, talented, Holy Spirit-gifted teachers, preachers, and leaders—whether female or male—from any capacity in the work of ministry. The scriptures remind us in Matthew 9:36-38, "When he saw the crowds, he had compassion for them, because they were harassed and helpless, like sheep without a shepherd. Then he said to his disciples, 'The harvest is plentiful, but the laborers are few; therefore, pray earnestly to the Lord of the harvest to send laborers into his harvest.'"

Opposition to women in church leadership often relies on a few misinterpreted phrases attributed to the Apostle Paul. These arguments are unfounded and ultimately futile. God chooses His leaders, and He elevates and diminishes them. Despite objections, God will continue using women in all church roles and capacities. This should be no surprise to any faithful Bible believer or reasonable scripture scholar. Women serving as leaders, pastors, and teachers are evidence of God's fulfillment of His word, as prophesied long ago. Their participation answers the prayers for laborers in the harvest, as recorded in Joel 2:17: "In the last days,' God says, 'I will pour out my Spirit upon all people. Your sons and daughters will prophesy. Your young men will see visions, and your old men will dream dreams."

THECLA

Thecla was a first-century Iconium woman born into a wealthy family. She heard the Apostle Paul preach during his first missionary journey to Asia Minor (Acts 13:51). She was engaged to be married to a young man of equal wealth and position until hearing Paul preach the gospel message from her bedroom window. After hearing the message, she only wanted to sit and learn at the apostle's feet.

For becoming a Christian, Tecla was subjected to drastic and unspeakable punishment from her family, which she endured and miraculously escaped.

Thecla forsook all the comforts of her class and station to serve Christ as an ascetic and missionary near Antioch. She led a dynamic preaching, teaching, healing, and baptism ministry there.

Basil and Gregory, two early church fathers, celebrated Thecla's ministry in Syria as a teaching and healing center. Thecla assumed the respected position of teacher and leader in the desert community.

Over time, the desert Christian communities became prosperous and remained centers of great learning and service, establishing an enduring legacy of female leaders in church history.

Outside of Ephesus, a mural of Thecla and Paul was recently excavated in an ancient church, illustrating her prominence in church history. She is a model of women in ministry in the early church.

"Preach the gospel at all times. And if necessary, use words."

— **St. Francis of Assisi**

1
WOMEN AS LEADERS

> **Judges 4:4-5,** "Deborah, the wife of Lappidoth, was a prophet who was judging Israel at that time. She would sit under the Palm of Deborah, between Ramah and Bethel in the hill country of Ephraim, and the Israelites would go to her for judgment."

Has God called women to be capable and effective leaders? This question has sparked a long and ongoing debate. However, we can find a resolution with minimal examination, fairness, and assessment. The capability and capacity for female leadership is demonstrated by the countless women worldwide who have made significant contributions across various industries. These women have earned the right, privilege, and respect to hold important positions in previously predominantly male-dominated fields. In both corporate and industrial settings, women have achieved distinguished titles and qualifications equal to those of their male counterparts.

Historically, questions surrounding female leadership have arisen from long-held beliefs that women are weaker, ill-suited for challenging tasks, and, at times, overly emotional or irrational. However, relying on predetermined assumptions and perceptions of capability based solely on gender has proven inaccurate. Evidence shows that these beliefs are unfounded. Women worldwide have demonstrated their potential, capacity, and ability to perform and excel beyond their competition.

Today, there are countless female leaders in cities, states, countries, and nations across the globe.

The effectiveness of women as leaders is well-established. Women have consistently demonstrated their leadership abilities, even when opportunities, voices, spaces, or agency have been denied. History is filled with evidence of strong, intelligent, capable, and gifted women in leadership roles.

Notable examples of female leadership include Queen Hatshepsut, who ruled during the 18th Dynasty of Egypt; Cleopatra, the last Pharaoh of Egypt during the 30th Dynasty; and Boudica, the leader of the British Celts. Other remarkable leaders include Wu Zetian, the only female Emperor of China; Queen Seondeok, the first female ruler of Korea; Vigdis Finnbogadottir, the first elected president of Iceland; Angela Merkel, the first female Chancellor of Germany; Margaret Thatcher, the United Kingdom's first female Prime Minister; Shirley Chisholm, the first African American woman to run for the presidency in the United States; and Kamala Harris, the first female Vice President of the United States.

The effectiveness of female leadership is clear and undeniable. Women have consistently demonstrated their ability, skill, and suitability for opportunities across all fields, disciplines, and industries. Currently, there is no area or industry where women have not proven their capacity, agency, and ability to perform and lead with equal skill and efficiency as their male counterparts.

David Scott

THE CHURCH

Women's leadership importance is evident in their successes across various industries. However, there are still institutions and organizations where opportunities are limited or significantly restricted. One notable area where women encounter challenges in obtaining leadership roles is within the church.

Despite advancements in scholarship and biblical interpretation across various denominations, many still believe that women should not hold leadership positions in the church, especially the official role of pastor. As a result, women have been systematically denied the opportunity for licensing, ordination, and respect as pastors in numerous churches. While some progress has been made, women still face unequal opportunities compared to their male counterparts.

For instance, women are currently denied ordination in the American Baptist Association, a respected network of autonomous congregations within the Baptist tradition in the United States and beyond, as well as in the Southern Baptist Convention, which comprises nearly 47,000 churches throughout the country and its territories. Other traditions that deny women ordination include the Evangelical Free Church of America, which traces its roots to the 19th-century revivals in Scandinavia; the Lutheran Church—Missouri Synod, which has close to 2 million members; the Presbyterian Church in America, founded in 1973; the Orthodox Presbyterian Church, established by J. Gresham Machen; the Orthodox Church, most prominent in Eastern Europe and Africa, which traces its origins to the first century; and the Roman Catholic Church, the largest denomination in Christianity, tracing its roots to the early generation of Christians, boasting between 1.28 to 1.39 billion baptized Catholics worldwide as of 2024.

Justifications for Barring Women from Ordination to the Pastorate

The justification for denying women ordination is based on the belief that the Word of God teaches that women do not have the obligation or responsibility to serve in the office of a pastor within the church. For many, this is supported by several passages:

1. "As in all the churches of the saints, the women should keep silent in the churches. For they are not permitted to speak but should be subordinate, as even the law says…what I am writing to you is a command of the Lord" (1 Corinthians 14:33–34, 37).

2. "Let a woman learn in silence with all submissiveness. I permit no woman to teach or to have authority over men; she is to keep silent" (1 Timothy 2:11–12).

3. "The saying is sure: If anyone aspires to the office of overseer, he desires a noble task. Now an overseer must be above reproach, the husband of one wife…" (1 Timothy 3:1–2).

4. "This is why I left you in Crete…that you might appoint elders in every town as I directed you, if any man is blameless, the husband of one wife…" (Titus 1:5–6).

While the earlier passages support the restriction of women's ordination, objections to female ordination may stem from a misinterpretation of the Apostle Paul's teachings in scripture. In many male-dominated circles, denying female ordination often serves as both a convenient excuse and a sign of intellectual laziness. Many individuals do not thoroughly research and analyze the Pauline epistles to truly understand the apostle's intent regarding church authority, leadership, ministry, and women's roles, opportunities, access, and responsibilities.

It is increasingly difficult to understand how anyone could perceive a woman as less capable than her male counterparts in any position of service to Christ. Historically, women have demonstrated their capability and efficiency in every context and role where they have been given the opportunity and access to perform. The church is no exception.

Records from various industries, institutions, and organizations show that women are equally efficient and effective as men in comparable roles. Many women have succeeded despite facing significant challenges in male-dominated fields, proving their capability to meet the demands of any endeavor. The results from numerous examples demonstrate that women only need the opportunity to prove their abilities. In every industry—including education, business, medicine, law, architecture, science, communications, retail, media, entrepreneurship, and military service—female representatives excel beyond their male counterparts.

Captain Kate Wilder made history in 1980 by becoming the first woman to complete the Special Forces Officer Course. However, the day before her graduation, she was summoned to the office of the head of the school and informed that she would not be allowed to graduate. Following an investigation, six months later, she was granted all the rights and privileges of the Green Beret after completing the course. When given a fair opportunity, women consistently rise to the occasion.

In August 2015, Captain Kristen Griest became the first woman to graduate from the prestigious Army Ranger School, earning the esteemed Ranger Tab and making history as the first female infantry officer. Alongside her, Captain Shaina Coss, one of the first ten women to receive the Ranger Tab, was the first female to command Rangers in combat. Since then, many other women have continued breaking barriers and exceeding expectations. Military records indicate that Ranger Class 03-22 celebrated its 100th female graduate, confirming she was the only woman in that class. Numerous women have since graduated from the Ranger Assessment Selection Program and served with the 75th Ranger Regiment. Currently, female Rangers and Green Berets are actively contributing to military operations.

JARENA LEE

(1783-1864)

In 1819, Jarena Lee became the first African American woman authorized to preach in the African Methodist Episcopal Church. She was also the first African American woman to publish an autobiography in the US. Eight years after Lee heard God calling her to preach, she convinced her pastor to let her behind the pulpit. She beseeched him, "If the man may preach, because the Savior died for him, why not the woman, seeing he died for her also? Is he not a whole Savior instead of half of one?"

Lee became a traveling preacher, moving from place to place on foot. She faced much opposition due to both her race and gender. In one year, she "traveled two thousand three hundred and twenty-five miles and preached one hundred and seventy-eight sermons."

"No one has a right to exercise sovereignty over the word of God. Yes, no human being, whoever he is, can rule over it. The word of God alone – without which nothing was made – should and must rule."

- Argula Von Grumbach (1492-1554)

"The will of God will not take us where the grace of God cannot sustain us."

— **Billy Graham**

2
PERMITTED SERVICE

> **Philippians 4:2-3**, "Now I appeal to Euodia and Syntyche. Please, because you belong to the Lord, settle your disagreement. And I ask you, my faithful partner, to help these two women, for they worked hard with me in telling others the Good News. They worked with Clement and my co-workers, whose names are written in the Book of Life."

Throughout various denominations, organized religion has often denied women key roles and positions within the church since its inception. While women have been allowed to serve, they are typically assigned roles that align with traditional views of their nurturing and caring nature. Typical roles include serving as teachers for women's groups, ministers of help, encouragers, worshippers, nurses, missionaries, deacons, teachers, and evangelists. In some cases, women have even been permitted to preach. However, regardless of their evident anointing and the magnitude of their spiritual gifts, women have generally not been allowed to serve as senior leaders or overseers.

Why?

Why haven't women been afforded the same privileges as their male counterparts within the church? The answer is simple. For centuries, many societies have been influenced by a pervasive patriarchal and masculine attitude. This mindset was prevalent during the time of the apostles and continued during the canonization of the scriptures.

The church has historically interpreted specific passages attributed to the Apostle Paul as reasons to deny women the opportunity to hold legitimate leadership positions, such as Pastor, Elder, or Bishop. A key reference used to support the long-held supposition is found in 1 Timothy 3:1-13, which states:

"If someone aspires to be an elder, he desires an honorable position. Therefore, an elder must be *a man* whose life is above reproach. *He* must be faithful to his wife, exercise self-control, live wisely, and maintain a good reputation. *He must* be hospitable and able to teach. Additionally, *he must not* be a heavy drinker or violent; rather, *he should be* gentle, not quarrelsome, and not greedy for money. An elder *must manage his family* well, ensuring his children respect and obey him. If *a man* cannot manage his household, how can he care for God's church? *He must not be* a new believer, as he might become proud, leading to a fall instigated by the devil. Furthermore, *he must be* well-regarded by those outside the church to avoid disgrace and falling into the devil's trap."

The words recorded in 1 Timothy are attributed to the Apostle Paul and have historically been used to disqualify women from the role of pastor. According to Paul's instructions to his protégé Timothy, whoever is chosen as the senior pastor (Bishop, Elder, Overseer), a man must hold the position. This person should have a good reputation, be a faithful husband, be hospitable and gentle, not be prone to drunkenness, be respected in his family, effectively manage his affairs, be free from greed, and be a good teacher of God's Word.

At first glance, it seems that the apostle limited the role and office to a specific gender, clearly outlining the qualifications for the office of the episkopos (Bishop, Overseer, Elder). However, could it be that the apostle was describing the desired qualities necessary for this office? It's possible that the Apostle Paul was speaking from his limited context as a first-century Jewish male, a Rabbi, an ex-Pharisee, and a traveling missionary and evangelist, without any frame of reference beyond his worldview. Is it possible that the words, if they are indeed the Apostle Paul's, are taken out of context?

Examining the words of the Apostle Paul

In an examination of these words attributed to the Apostle Paul to the young Timothy, it is apparent that what Paul said was that anyone desiring to be a leader in the Lord's church (Bishop, Overseer, Elder), that person should have specific qualifications, and deacons should possess parallel qualifications. It is reasonable to conclude that the Apostle Paul did not offer this as an absolute and total requirement. However, the apostle conveyed to his protégé Timothy that when you meet or encounter men who desire these offices, you should use these identified character standards when selecting those to serve and lead the church. At no time does Paul say that a woman could not request to, aspire to, or hold this office.

It is challenging to definitively claim that leadership in the church is restricted solely to men. The Apostle Paul indicated that bishops and deacons should be selected based on the same character standards. When he writes to Timothy that a deacon, like an elder, must be faithful to his wife, it implies that the leader must be a man. However, scripture identifies Phoebe as a "Diakonos," which translates to deacon or deaconess. In Romans 16:1-2, Paul states, "I commend to you our sister Phoebe, a servant of the church in Cenchrea. I ask you to receive her in the Lord in a way worthy of the saints and to give her any help she may need from you, for she has been a great help to many people, including me."

The fact that a woman was a deacon forces us to reconsider long-held beliefs and ideas. If the requirements for both the deacon and the elder are the same, and if either office were reserved only for men, how is it that Phoebe is recognized as a deacon? One can only conclude that the Apostle Paul did not imply that women could not serve as leaders in the Lord's church.

For the sake of bias, some refer to Phoebe as a "diakonos" instead of a "diakonia." Using the term "diakonos," Phoebe's role in the church is limited to that of a servant. This interpretation suggests that her responsibilities were confined to serving at the command of those above her. Her duties would have been restricted to assisting in the administration of Christian care, particularly in meeting needs through the collection or distribution of charity and preparing and presenting food. However, this translation is inaccurate.

Phoebe was not merely a servant who served others by preparing food. On the contrary, the more accurate word to describe Phoebe's role and function is "Diakonia," which aligns her duties more with service and ministering, especially those who execute the commands of others, those who, by the command of God, proclaim and promote religion among men, the office of the apostles and its administration, the office of prophets, evangelists, elders, etc.

Without examining the apostle's statements, it is often easy to misunderstand or misinterpret his intent or meaning. Even the Apostle Peter commented in 2 Peter 3:16. "He writes the same way in all his letters…His letters contain some things that are hard to understand, which ignorant and unstable people distort, as they do the other Scriptures, to their destruction."

In Romans 16: 3-4, the apostle says, "Greet Priscilla and Aquila, my fellow workers in Christ Jesus. They risked their lives for me. Not only I but all the churches of the Gentiles are grateful to them." Without close examination, it is easy to overlook that Paul mentions Priscilla before Aquila in his commendation. This is no accident on the apostle's part. On the contrary, this is uncommon. It can be assumed that either Priscilla worked harder to distinguish herself as worthy of greater esteem and honor than Aquila, or Paul recognized her more remarkable leadership ability among the two.

In verse 7, Paul says, "Greet Andronicus and Junia, my relatives who have been imprisoned with me. They are outstanding among the apostles and were in Christ before I was." In this statement, Paul undeniably states that leadership is not limited to men. He tells us that both a male (Andronicus) and a female (Junia) were not only apostles but outstanding among all the apostles.

The recognition of Junia as an apostle poses a challenge for many people to accept. To address this issue, some men have deliberately sought to distort, alter, and change the translation of the Greek text. They have manipulated the wording in modern biblical translations and even replaced the female name Junia with the masculine Junias, even though the masculine name does not appear in ancient manuscripts. In contrast, Junia is found over one hundred and fifty times. Despite attempts to deny, distort, or erase the evidence, it remains true that Junia was a woman apostle, even though she was not one of the twelve.

In the first century of the Christian church, it was clear to all readers that the Apostle Paul described Andronicus and Junia as apostles. The early church father John Chrysostom wrote, "Greet Andronicus and Junia… who are outstanding among the apostles." Being an apostle is a significant honor, but to be described as outstanding among the apostles is truly remarkable! Their outstanding status was based on their deeds and virtuous actions. Indeed, Junia's wisdom must have been immense for her to be recognized with the title of apostle.

If Paul is used to support the indictment against women in leadership positions, then it should also be Paul who advocates for the liberation these women deserve and are entitled to. Although many may hold strong beliefs stemming from longstanding and widely accepted church practices, it was by his words that Paul acknowledged the reality of female apostles, such as Junia.

Junia was indeed an apostle. However, the knowledge of her existence could have been lost without the ancient and preserved records. Historically, there have been many female leaders in the church, and by the will of God, there will be many more in the future. Phoebe and Junia serve as prominent examples of women in the early church. I am confident that they are not the only ones who have held positions of prominence and leadership, even though they are among the few whose contributions have been recorded and preserved in early church history.

The writer says in Galatians 3:26-28 "For ye are all the children of God by faith in Christ Jesus. For as many of you as have been baptized into Christ have put on Christ. There is neither Jew nor Greek nor bond nor free; there is neither male nor female: for ye are all one in Christ Jesus."

SOJOURNER TRUTH (ISABELLA BAUMFREE)

(1797-1883)

Isabella Baumfree, also known as Sojourner Truth, was born into slavery in New York. Throughout her life, she was sold multiple times and endured beatings, as well as separation from her children. After emancipation, she became a devout Christian and co-founded the Kingston Methodist Church. 1843, she adopted Sojourner Truth to reflect her divine calling to travel and preach. She told her friends, "The Spirit calls me, and I must go."

Sojourner Truth spoke powerfully about the abolition of slavery. She is recognized in Smithsonian magazine's "100 Most Significant Americans of All Time" list and is honored annually in the calendars of saints of the Episcopal and Lutheran Churches.

DAVID SCOTT

"And what if you save (under God) but one soul?"

- Selina Hastings (1707-1791)

"Preach as if you had seen heaven and its celestial inhabitants, and had hovered over the bottomless pit, and beheld the tortures, and heard the groans of the damned."

— **Francis Asbury**

3

MEN AND WOMEN MUST PREACH!

> **1 Peter 4:10-11**, "God has given each of you a gift from his great variety of spiritual gifts. Use them well to serve one another. Do you have the gift of speaking? Then speak as though God himself were speaking through you. Do you have the gift of helping others? Do it with all the strength and energy that God supplies. Then, everything you do will bring glory to God through Jesus Christ. All glory and power to him forever and ever! Amen."

What does it mean to preach? The Greek word for "preach" or "preaching" is "euaggelizo," which translates to "to proclaim the good news." Preaching involves announcing and declaring a message. All followers, ministers, and servants of Christ are called to fulfill this role. Every believer must share the good news of Jesus with every living creature.

What is the good news that all followers of Christ are called to "preach" and share? The message that must be proclaimed to the world is that Jesus of Nazareth died on the cross at Calvary (Golgotha) more than 2,000 years ago for the sins of all humanity. He was crucified, buried in a borrowed tomb belonging to Joseph of Arimathea, and rose from the grave on the third day, victorious over death. His death has freed all men and women from the penalty that sin demands. As a result of His kindness and compassion, Jesus paid the debt that no one else could pay. In the place of imperfect humanity, the Son of God willingly hung and died on a rugged cross—guiltless, blameless, spotless, and perfect.

Because of His love, Christ died so that humanity could live. His death was essential for the redemption of mankind. All who believe in Him and His sacrificial work on the cross have the promise of eternal life. Although they will physically die, they can have confidence that they will live again. This is good news for the entire world—a message that all men and women are eager to hear, even if many are blind to it and unaware. As ministers and ambassadors of God, his followers are commanded to share this good news with anyone willing to listen. Servants of God must proclaim to the world that a Savior lives to make intercession for the lost.

Among all the professions one can pursue, none is greater than that of a preacher. No other vocation has as profound and lasting an impact on those who hear, receive, and respond to the message of Christ. Preachers are oracles of God. Their mission and function is to share and spread His message and proclaim the eternal truths revealed in His infallible word. While many are called, only a few are chosen to speak on behalf of God. To serve God in this capacity is an honor and privilege. The scripture in Romans 10:15 states, "And how shall they preach (or proclaim) unless they are sent? As it is written, How Beautiful are the feet of those who PREACH THE GOSPEL OF PEACE and bring glad tidings of good things!"

Jesus came into the world to save those who are desperate, depraved, and lost. He came so that everyone who believes, trusts, and hopes in Him can be saved from the wrath that awaits an unbelieving world. Because of this truth, God desires for men and women everywhere to hear the message of salvation. This message is meant for the lost, the unchurched, and those unaware of their condition and need for redemption from their sins. They learn and discover their need for redemption only through the preached Word of God. Without a preacher, no one will hear. Therefore, the world needs preachers!

The need for preachers and the preached word cannot be overstated or overemphasized because the world needs a Savior and redemption from sin that only comes through Christ Jesus. In Matthew 28:18-20, Jesus did not suggest but commanded his disciples, saying, "I have been given all authority in heaven and on earth. Go and make disciples of all nations, baptizing them in the name of the Father, the Son, and the Holy Spirit. Teach these new disciples to obey all the commands I have given you." No one can be saved without knowing and accepting Jesus as Lord and Savior. Morality, benevolence, charity, or kindness cannot substitute for the atoning blood and sacrifice of Jesus Christ. Without Christ, men and women are lost. They will die in their sins, apart from God. Without a preacher, none understand that only the shed blood of Christ can cover the debt owed for sin.

Even today, far too many people have never heard the gospel message. They do not know that without making the personal decision to receive Christ Jesus into their hearts, they are lost and separated from God. Many are unaware that a Savior is willing and waiting to save and reconcile everyone back to God. Furthermore, many have never encountered the words from Romans 10:12-13: "For there is no difference between the Jew and the Greek; for the same Lord over all is rich unto all who call upon Him. Whosoever shall call upon the name of the Lord shall be saved."

Men and women must hear this message—eternal souls are at stake. With all diligence and determination, the call of God must proclaim the message of Christ to all men and women everywhere. There is no time to waste. Romans 10:14 asks the vital question: "How shall they call on Him, whom they have not believed? And how shall they believe in Him of whom they have not heard? And how shall they hear without a preacher?" There must be preachers committed to proclaiming the message and truth about Christ, no matter the cost!

In the Great Commission, Jesus does not present His mission as an option; He commands us to "Go and teach all nations." He instructs His followers to share the message that the Messiah is alive, reigning on the throne forever, and capable of saving everyone from their sins, habits, and addictions, provided they believe, hope, and trust in Him. Both men and women are called to preach the Gospel. Neither Satan nor our Savior shows favoritism; Satan seeks to kill and destroy all, while Christ Jesus aims to rescue, redeem, and save everyone.

In Christ, all are equal. There is one Lord, one God, and one Spirit. The true and living God is that Spirit. 1 Corinthians 1:18, 21 states, "For the preaching of the cross is to them that perish foolishness: but unto us which are saved, it is the power of God" and "It pleased God by the foolishness of preaching to save them that believe." Men and women of God must not allow anything to prevent them from fulfilling their calling.

There is no more extraordinary privilege than preaching the gospel. As the Lord's emissaries, we must ensure our calling is genuine. Those who are called and chosen must share the message. Whether we are male or female, we must inform everyone that without accepting Jesus as their personal Savior, they are lost and destined for eternal separation from God. We all must proclaim that Jesus is the only way to eternal salvation.

The preacher is responsible for communicating Christ's words in John 14:6: "I am the way, the truth, and the life: no man cometh to the Father but by me." Jesus is the only path to salvation—there is no other. There must be preachers.

When it comes to the message and truth of the tremendous and miraculous plan of salvation, God is not concerned with the gender of the messenger. What matters more to the Savior is the preacher's willingness and availability. God desires that the message be proclaimed and shared by all who are courageous enough to do so. He wants none to perish or be lost. John 3 verses 16-17 reads, "For God so loved the world, that he gave his only begotten Son, that whosoever believeth in him should not perish, but have everlasting life. For God sent not his Son into the world to condemn the world; but that the world through him might be saved".

Many people have never heard the message of Christ and His wonderful gift of salvation, which is available to all. There is a need for preachers! If there are no preachers, how shall they call on Him in whom they have not believed? How will they believe in Him whom they have not heard? How shall they hear without a preacher? As the Lord's female and male ambassadors, we have no choice but to spread this message. We all must PREACH!

Paul's message to the young Timothy in 2 Timothy 4:2, 5 emphasizes the urgency and profound importance of preaching. The Apostle Paul instructs Timothy: "Preach the word of God. Be prepared, whether the time is favorable or not. Patiently correct, rebuke, and encourage your people with good teaching. You should keep a clear mind in every situation. Don't be afraid of suffering for the Lord. Work at telling others the Good News, and fully carry out the ministry God has given you."

Both men and women are called to preach the gospel of Jesus. Souls are at stake, and there is no time for foolishness or division among ministers based solely on gender or denomination. If there is any concern or disagreement about who should or should not preach, God Himself will resolve that issue in His timing. We must never forget that it is God's church, God's word, God's kingdom, and God's vineyard. In the "Parable of the Tares," recorded in Matthew 13:30, Jesus said, "Let both grow together until the harvest. Then I will tell the harvesters to sort out the weeds, tie them into bundles, burn them, and put the wheat in the barn."

Desiring that none should perish or be lost, God has called men and women to preach the kingdom of God and redemption through Christ. Just as it was two thousand years ago, people desperately need a Savior today. Recognizing this need, Jesus said to his disciples in Matthew 9:37-38, "The harvest is great, but the workers are few. So, pray to the Lord who oversees the harvest; ask him to send more workers into his fields." Both men and women are those laborers. Because the eternal souls of many are at stake, we must collectively preach the unadulterated, uncompromised, and life-changing gospel of Jesus Christ! There is no more excellent task or vocation than preaching. As those called and chosen by God, both men and women must preach!

PHOEBE PALMER

(1807-1875)

Phoebe Palmer, born into a devout Methodist family in New York, felt a conflict between her peaceful relationship with God and a desire for something more profound. After losing two young children, she came to believe this loss was a punishment for not fully dedicating herself to God. She realized, "The error of my religious life has been a desire for signs and wonders… unwilling to rely on the still, small voice of the Spirit." Ultimately, she found that surrendering her life to God provided her with assurance of her salvation.

After gaining spiritual insight, she and her sister started ecumenical women's prayer meetings, which spread nationwide. Palmer became a leading figure in America's fastest-growing religious movement, organizing camp meetings that led to around 25,000 conversions to Christianity. Her theology of the "altar covenant" significantly influenced the founding of several denominations, including the Church of the Nazarene and The Salvation Army. By 1867, her book, "The Way of Holiness," had been published in fifty-two editions.

"The church of Christ is His body. He purchased the church with His own blood. He has promised that the gates of hell shall never overcome the church. You ask me if the church of Christ will be destroyed. How could it be, in the light of all these great promises?"

- Jeanette Li (1899-1968)

"A charge to keep I have, A God to glorify; A never-dying soul to save and fit it for the sky."

—**Charles Wesley**

4

WHY DO WOMEN PREACH?

> **Acts 2:16-18**, "What you see was predicted long ago by the prophet Joel: In the last days,' God says, I will pour out my Spirit upon all people. Your sons and daughters will prophesy. Your young men will see visions, and your old men will dream dreams. In those days, I will pour out my Spirit even on my servants—men and women alike—and they will prophesy."

Women become preachers primarily because of their unwavering confidence that God has called them and instilled in them a deep desire to serve Him by sharing His word with those who are lost. There is no other plausible or logical explanation for this choice. No one, male or female, would willingly take on the life of a preacher without a divine calling. The vocation of a preacher is often lonely and isolating, lacking fame, wealth, and recognition. Following Christ requires humility, scrutiny, and enduring endless criticism.

Unless divine involvement is involved, there is no reason a woman would want to preach. Why would she subject herself to unnecessary ridicule, harassment, disrespect, and rejection? Long viewed and regarded as the weaker vessel, historically, any effort and steps toward advancement or entry into nontraditional or male-dominated spaces have repeatedly met with disdain, resentment, and hostility. Again, why would a woman want or choose to be a preacher? Why would she choose to be disliked, hated, and the focus of many of her male counterparts' fury, often for no other reason than being a woman and having what some regard as unreasonable stubbornness and courage? Unless God is the motivation and spirit empowering women in the work and vocation of preaching the gospel message, no woman would willingly choose to participate among throngs of egotistical, chauvinistic, unsympathetic, and, at times, insane males. Women who preach undeterred, unshaken, and unyielding are those called and convinced that God has chosen them and are committed to the great commission of winning souls for the kingdom of God.

The woman preacher has chosen to follow the Lord Jesus and willingly endures suffering for her obedience. She offers her body as a living sacrifice to God, considering it holy and acceptable—this she recognizes as her reasonable service. She believes this is a worthy price to pay for the privilege of serving in the ministry of the Lord Jesus Christ. Who has the right to question her claim if she genuinely follows and obeys what she understands to be Christ's call and command? She should be allowed, without harassment or interference, to demonstrate the validity of her calling and convictions.

No man can hinder a woman's work or ministry if God has called her. God will support her because she is not acting on her authority or being swayed by outside influences. If God is for and with her, He will continue to lead, empower, and work through her. No one can stop the work or ministry that God has initiated.

When claims are made that her work is demonic or of the devil, we should remember Jesus's words: "Any kingdom divided by civil war is doomed. A town or family splintered by feuding will fall apart. And if Satan is casting out Satan, he is divided and fighting against himself. His kingdom will not survive" (Matthew 12:25-26).

Women preach because they are called and commanded by God. The spirit and power of the living God empower them. This same spirit, which many of their male counterparts affirm, has also called them. If a woman preacher's ministry is genuine and authentic, those seeking to oppose, hinder, or stop her work are not merely resisting her but ultimately opposing God himself.

Preaching and serving the Lord Jesus often bring little fame, fortune, or celebrity. Those called to this service, regardless of gender, recognize the sacrifices involved. Both men and women must surrender everything without exception. Women preachers are exceptionally aware of this requirement. They do not preach for recognition, fame, celebrity, or financial gain; instead, they preach because of the Lord's command to "Go and teach all nations."

Like their male counterparts, women preachers are dedicated to fulfilling the Great Commission of the Lord Jesus Christ. Their classification as the so-called "weaker gender" should not affect how others perceive their abilities, gifts, anointing, calling, or motives. The words of the Apostle Paul in Philippians 1:14-15 illuminate this point: "Because of my imprisonment, many of the Christians here (and abroad) have gained confidence and become bold in telling others about Christ. Some preach out of jealousy and rivalry, but others preach about Christ with pure motives. They preach because they love me, for they know the Lord brought me here to defend the Good News. Those others do not have pure motives as they preach about Christ… But whether or not their motives are pure, the fact remains that the message about Christ is being preached, so I rejoice."

Followers and disciples of the Lord Jesus are commanded to spread the message of Christ everywhere, in every place, and to all people. This is a mandate from the Messiah himself. God is not concerned about who delivers the message or the reasons behind its delivery. As evident in the words of the Apostle Paul in Philippians, the gender of the messenger is ultimately irrelevant; what truly matters is the proclamation of Jesus Christ.

ANTOINETTE BROWN BLACKWELL

(1825-1921)

Antoinette Blackwell, from Rochester, New York, was gifted as a child and began preaching at nine. After teaching for four years to save money, she enrolled in Oberlin College, one of the first to offer theology training for women. Despite this, her degree was delayed for years due to discrimination against women in ministry.

Antoinette Blackwell was a prolific writer and preacher who became the first woman ordained by a major American Protestant denomination in 1853. She preached until 1915 and was an abolitionist and early feminist, writing on women's rights and equality.

"In everything we do, let us put our trust in God. We may have faith that He will guide us through any storm, no matter how fierce. With His strength, we can overcome any obstacle that stands in our way."

-Jarena Lee (1783-1864)

"The Spirit calls me, and I must go!"

—Sojourner Truth

5
THE CALL TO PREACH

> **Jeremiah 1:9**, "Then the Lord reached out and touched my mouth and said, "Look, I have put my words in your mouth!"

God does not call the qualified; instead, He qualifies and equips those He calls. Who is called is made solely by God, not by people. No matter how right we think we are or how confident we feel about our choices regarding someone's gender, talent, charisma, or ministry ability, as mere mortals, we have no authority to determine or deny anyone's participation in serving or being part of the ministry of the Lord Jesus Christ.

It is arrogant to assume we know exactly what God desires, plans, and wills. Christ knows the heart and chooses whom He wills. Every attempt by mankind to impose limitations on God is misguided. He chooses whoever He deems fit for His service, regardless of that person's education, background, or gender.

The writer of Job 11:7-10 asks, "Can you solve the mysteries of God? Can you discover everything about the Almighty? Such knowledge is higher than the heavens—what do you know? It is deeper than the underworld—what do you understand? It is broader than the earth and wider than the sea. If God comes and puts a person in prison or calls the court to order, who can stop Him?" No one knows the mind of God.

Despite popular belief, God holds no biases. God does not think like humans; He is not egotistical and is not intimidated by anything or anyone. God uses everything to ultimately bring Himself glory and fulfill His divine purposes, goals, and objectives. He has always involved women in His service and has never shown bias or disregard for the female gender. It is men who have often assumed what God intended regarding women's roles in ministry. The Bible is filled with accounts of women God chose to use for His purpose, and these are only the ones that have been recorded.

Women preachers are a fulfillment of biblical prophecy. The writer said in Joel 2:28 and Acts 2:17-18. The Bible declares that women will prophesy. According to Young's Concordance (p. 780), both the Hebrew word (Nebrah) and the Greek word (Proph) for prophetess mean "female preacher." The term "prophet" refers to a public expounder, while "prophesy" means to speak or flow forth. Both Old and New Testament prophets and prophetesses served as proclaimers of God's Word.

From the very beginning, God called and used women as preachers. The Old Testament provides clear examples of this. One of the most outstanding female leaders of Israel was Deborah. According to Judges 4:4-5, Deborah served as a judge for civil and criminal cases. The children of Israel came to her for judgment, and she was the chief ruler of Israel for 40 years, giving orders to generals and the army. She fulfilled the roles of an evangelist, prophetess, judge, and preacher. God granted her authority over the mighty (Judges 5:13).

In addition to Deborah, the Bible identifies other women used by God and chosen for His purpose and service. Miriam, mentioned in Exodus 15:20, Numbers 12:1, and Micah 6:4, was a prophetess and a song leader in Israel. According to 2 Kings 22:14, five men approached a woman named Huldah to consult her. She spoke to a congregation of men about the Book of the Law. This woman preached to a gathering of men, and her message was taken to the nation, resulting in a revival.

Much like the Old Testament, the New Testament features women who were called to serve as preachers. Notably, a woman, specifically Anna, delivered the first message of Christ's Resurrection, as mentioned in Luke 2:36-38. Anna lived in the temple and likely prophesied there. Additionally, Acts 21:9 tells us that Philip the evangelist had four daughters who prophesied.

Women also played significant roles in assisting Paul during his early ministry. For instance, Priscilla (also known as Prisca) aided Paul and even taught Apollos the way of the Lord more accurately. In Romans 16:1-2, Paul commended Phoebe to the church in Rome, asking them to support her in her business. Phoebe was a key assistant to Paul in his ministry and delivered the Book of Romans on his behalf.

No specific requirements or qualifications are needed to receive a call from God. God chooses by His standards. He does not look at external appearances; He examines the heart. God's decisions are made based on His infinite knowledge. The Apostle Paul affirms this by stating, "I was made a minister of the gospel." God's plan and will chose him. All male and female preachers must respond to the call and diligently meet the duties and requirements of their vocation. God is looking for willing and available people. He has no preference regarding gender. Jesus said in Matthew 9:37, "The harvest is truly plenteous, but the laborers are few; Pray ye, therefore, the Lord of the harvest send forth laborers into his harvest." Women preachers are such laborers.

Woman vs. Men

When God looks for a vessel, rarely is gender a factor. Consistently, His concern remains with willingness and availability. It is the will of God that souls are saved, those in darkness are brought to light, and the broken be mended and reconciled to God. This is the heart of God. Though no man can fully know the mind of God, this position is reasonably established by the words in John 3:16, "For God so loved the world that he gave his only begotten son that whosoever believeth in him should not perish but have everlasting (eternal) life."

More than anything else, God desires that lost and dying men and women hear and receive the gospel of the Lord Jesus Christ. Is gender a factor or limitation for those who preach or proclaim the gospel of Christ? I think not! God has given all that come to him the power and authority to become his children, and he has done away with division and separation. The writer makes it inarguably clear in Galatians 3:26-28, "You are all sons of God through faith in Christ Jesus, for all of you who were baptized into Christ have clothed yourselves with Christ. There is neither Jew nor Greek, slave nor free, male nor female, for you are all one in Christ Jesus."

As mere mortals and fallible men, when we dare question and challenge the validity and legitimacy of another's ministry because of gender, we must remember that God has not made either of us "*Gospel Police*." We are not called to be judges but fruit inspectors. We have the right to examine the fruit that a tree bears. If the fruit of the tree is righteous and brings honor to God, we should be satisfied if God is glorified. We are all servants. We must never forget that neither of us has heaven or hell to send or condemn anyone. God alone is the final judge. God is greater than any man's thoughts, ideas, and opinions. He knows how to defend his kingdom and his word. The writer reminds us in 1 Corinthians 1:25, 27-29, "The foolishness of God is wiser than man's wisdom, and the weakness of God is stronger than man's strength... But God chose the world's foolish things to shame the wise and the weak things of the world to shame the strong. He chose the lowly things of this world and the despised things--and the things that are not--to nullify the things that are so that no one may boast before him."

AMANDA BERRY SMITH

(1837-1915)

Amanda Smith was born in Maryland to a slave who managed to purchase his family's freedom. The Berry family then resettled in Pennsylvania, where they became a station on the Underground Railroad.

After becoming a Christian, she joined the African Methodist Episcopal Church and received her call to preach in 1869. Known for her inspiring sermons and beautiful singing voice, she became a popular speaker from Maine to Tennessee. In 1878, she became the first Black woman international evangelist, working in England, Ireland, Scotland, India, and parts of Africa for twelve years.

"Don't bother to give God instructions; just report for duty."

–Corrie Ten Boom (1892-1983)

"The power in the gospel does not lie in the preacher's eloquence...Nor does it lie in the preacher's learning... It lies in the Holy Ghost."

—**Charles Spurgeon**

6
WORK OF THE HOLY SPIRIT

> **1 Corinthian 2:13**, "When we tell you these things, we do not use words that come from human wisdom. Instead, we speak words given to us by the Spirit, using the Spirit's words to explain spiritual truths."

Nothing can be achieved for Christ without the work of the Holy Spirit. But what exactly is the Holy Spirit? The Holy Spirit is the source of all power and embodies the essence of the one true and righteous God. The same power raised Jesus from the dead, creating and shaping galaxies and worlds. The Holy Spirit is the great and awe-inspiring power of Yahweh, the triune God.

The Holy Spirit is essential for ministry work; without it, one cannot successfully fulfill the plan and will of God. This is why the scriptures record specific instructions to the disciples in Acts 1:4-5: "Once when he was eating with them, he commanded them, "Do not leave Jerusalem until the Father sends you the gift he promised, as I told you before. John baptized with water, but in just a few days you will be baptized with the Holy Spirit." Jesus advised his chosen disciples, who were called to the work of ministry, to "wait until the Holy Spirit comes upon you; you will receive power from on high."

The Holy Spirit empowers and assists believers in living according to God's planned will and purpose. God grants the Holy Spirit to all who believe in and follow Him without any limitations based on gender; this gift is freely given to everyone. Those who seek to fulfill God's will—advancing His kingdom and calling the lost to come to Christ and leave their darkness behind—must be empowered by the Holy Spirit. Without the Holy Spirit, ministry efforts are ineffective and lack the power to change and transform lives.

The Holy Spirit amplifies the preached Word, enabling it to have the intended impact by convicting those who hear it from God's chosen vessels. The Apostle Paul states in Romans 8:9, "Remember that those who do not have the Spirit of Christ living in them do not belong to Him at all." The Holy Spirit is impartial; all who have received the Holy Spirit are endowed with power.

The Bible illustrates this truth in Acts 19:13-20, which recounts: "Some itinerant Jewish exorcists tried to invoke the name of the Lord Jesus over those possessed by evil spirits, saying, 'We command you by Jesus, whom Paul preaches.' Among these exorcists were the seven sons of Sceva, a Jewish chief priest. The evil spirit responded, 'Jesus I know, and Paul I recognize, but who are you?' Then, the man with the evil spirit jumped on them, overpowered them, and prevailed against them. As a result, they fled out of that house naked and wounded."

God generously grants the Holy Spirit to everyone who believes without showing any bias or favoritism. As mentioned in Mark 16:17-18, "These signs will accompany those who believe: In my name, they will cast out demons, speak in new tongues, take up serpents, and if they drink anything deadly, it will not harm them. They will lay hands on the sick, and they will recover."

Those filled with the Spirit of God feel a strong compulsion to preach and share His truth. Regardless of the messenger, the Spirit only conveys what is true and good about God. According to Scripture, the Spirit bears witness to Jesus Christ and no one else. When a person is filled with the Holy Spirit, they are motivated to spread the message of Christ. God does not show favoritism; He will use anyone willing and available. As Scripture proclaims, "In God, there is neither Jew nor Greek, bond nor free, male nor female; all are one in Christ."

MARIA WOODWORTH-ETTER

(1844-1924)

At the age of thirteen, Maria Woodworth-Etter converted to Christianity. Jesus called her to "go out into the highways and hedges and gather in the lost sheep." However, her denomination prohibited her from engaging in public ministry, so she sought support from a local Quaker meeting.

In 1885, she started preaching and praying for the sick, attracting large crowds that led her to buy an 8,000-seat tent. She founded the Assemblies of God church in 1914 and established Lakeview Church in Indianapolis in 1918.

In 1916, Maria Woodworth-Etter preached, "God is calling Marys and Marthas across our land to work in His vineyard. May they respond, "Lord, here am I. Send me." Dear sister in Christ, may the Spirit of God empower you to fulfill the work He has assigned to you."

"I cannot imagine any better argument for women ministers in all of scripture than Mary, who quite literally bore the Word-Made-Flesh in her own body and gave birth to him. She carried God around in her belly and then labored to get that Good News out of her womb and into the world; if that's not an accurate depiction of preaching, I don't know what is."

-Rev. Kyndall Rae Rothaus (ca. 1985-).

"You have one business on earth – to save souls."

—John Wesley

7

WHAT DID PAUL (REALLY) SAY?

> **2 Peter 3:15-16,** "Our Lord's patience gives people time to be saved. Our beloved brother Paul also wrote this to you with the wisdom God gave him— speaking of these things in all his letters. Some of his comments are hard to understand, and those who are ignorant and unstable have twisted his letters to mean something entirely different, just as they do with other parts of Scripture. And this will result in their destruction."

When reading the Pauline epistles, many often forget that Paul's letters were written to specific churches with problems unique to those congregations. In 1 Timothy 2:11-15, words attributed to the apostle read, "Women should learn quietly and submissively. I do not let women teach men or have authority over them. Let them listen quietly. God made Adam first, and afterward, he made Eve. And it was not Adam whom Satan deceived. The woman was deceived, and sin was the result. But women will be saved through childbearing, assuming they continue to live in faith, love, holiness, and modesty." However, Paul's perceived injunction against women having the pre-eminence over a man should be observed in the light of Corinth's history.

When Paul wrote his letter, Corinth was a thriving cosmopolitan center. It was an international trading port and often the meeting ground for different cults and pagan religions. Oddly, most worshippers and followers in these pagan religions and practices were women. As a result, this led to the idea and belief that women were more open to the controlling influence of the pagan god's spirit.

It's important to note that Paul's writings addressed specific issues within the Corinthian church. Historically, and during this time, women held prominent status in many of the pagan cults of Bacchus, Dionysus, Apollo, Hermes, Venus-Fortuna, Isis, and Aphrodite, which led many of them, after converting to Christianity, to believe they had a closer connection to God than the men in the congregation. Observing this confusion, Paul sought to correct the practices within the church at Corinth.

In 1 Corinthians 11:3-16, regarding public worship, Paul states that the head of every man is Christ, the head of a woman is man, and the head of Christ is God. A man dishonors his head by covering it while praying, while a woman dishonors hers if she prays without a head covering, which is like shaving her head. If she refuses to wear one, she should cut her hair, but it is shameful for a woman to do so. He says men should not cover their heads in worship, as they reflect God's glory, whereas women reflect man's glory. Since the first woman came from a man, she is meant to wear a covering to signify her authority. Paul also emphasizes that men and women are interdependent: while the first woman came from man, every man is born of a woman, and all comes from God. He asks if it's proper for a woman to pray publicly without a covering, noting that long hair is a woman's glory, given to her as a covering. He concludes that this is the custom of the churches, and there is no other. In his letter, Paul instructed the newly converted women to keep their heads covered, as women associated with the pagan cults often danced with their heads uncovered and sometimes topless.

According to 1 Corinthians 14:34-35, the Apostle Paul says, "Let the women keep silent in the churches; for they are not permitted to speak, but must subject themselves, just as the Law also says. And if they desire to learn anything, let them ask their husbands at home, for it is improper for a woman to speak in church." At first reading, it is possible to misinterpret and fail to understand the meaning of this passage.

Upon closer examination, it becomes clear that the women mentioned in this passage are not addressing the assembly in a leadership role. Instead, they ask questions while seated in the congregation, disrupting the proceedings. The Apostle Paul suggests these questions should be asked at home after the service.

In this specific passage, the Greek verb translated as "speak" is *laleo*, which emphasizes the act of speaking rather than the content of what is said. He would have used a different verb if the apostle intended to forbid women from preaching. Instead, he employs the Greek verb that translates to "remain silent," which signifies refraining from talking out of respect. This is like how we avoid disruptive chatting during weekly prayers or sermons today.

The passage emphasizes that, like everyone else, women must follow the church's rules of order and procedure. The focus is on maintaining order during the service rather than addressing the inherent value of women, their qualifications for church leadership, or the topic of ordination. Specifically, this passage deals with the issue of speaking out of turn in church. Therefore, it can be concluded that Paul is asserting that it is inappropriate for women to disrupt the service by asking questions of other congregants. Instead, they should refrain from speaking during the service and save their questions afterward, when their husbands can provide explanations in a more suitable setting.

The women in Corinth disrupted the conversation with their chatter, leading to widespread agreement with Paul's advice. Any attempt to interpret this text differently would be an example of eisegesis, which involves forcing the text to convey a meaning other than initially intended. This approach contrasts with exegesis, which focuses on contextual understanding of the passage. Exegesis includes comparing it with different parts of scripture and considering the language and customs of the time to grasp the original message the writer intended to convey.

In 1 Timothy 2:11-15, the Apostle Paul states, "I do not permit a woman to teach or to have authority over a man," which has sparked significant debate within the Christian community for many years. To fully understand this passage, it is essential to recognize that Paul addressed specific women-related issues in Ephesus. When we examine 1 Timothy 2:9-15, it becomes clear that Paul was guiding the young Timothy on handling certain heretical teachings and practices involving women, particularly within the context of the church in Ephesus.

When examining 1 Timothy 3:1-13, the qualifications outlined primarily targeted male leadership in the first-century church. However, when women were considered for similar roles, such as apostle or deacon, they were also expected to meet the same standards of character, integrity, and personal conduct. Just as Junia, the female apostle, Phoebe would have been held to these criteria.

Although it may be challenging for some to accept, Paul was not particularly opposed to women in leadership roles within the early church. The idea that Paul was against women or held extreme misogynistic views is inconsistent with the overall message of the biblical text. Numerous passages and statements from Paul affirm that women served as his equals and co-laborers in ministry. No scripture suggests that a woman's place, role, or function is less significant than that of Paul's or other church leaders. On the contrary, the Apostle Paul frequently praised women for their service, loyalty, and commitment to the faith. Because of Paul's many affirming and supportive statements regarding women, there is ongoing debate about the authorship of some writings attributed to him, with some believing other authors wrote them.

Those who believe that Paul opposed women holding leadership positions must overlook references to women like Junia, a female apostle mentioned in the book of Romans. They would also need to impose contextual limitations on Galatians 3:28, where Paul writes, "There is neither Jew nor Greek, neither bond nor free, neither male nor female: for you are all one in Christ Jesus." Paul was a profound scholar and pastoral theologian. Historical records show that his words were often misinterpreted and misunderstood. The Apostle Peter supports this in 2 Peter 3:15-16, who states, "Our beloved brother Paul, according to the wisdom given to him, also wrote to you, speaking of these things as he does in all his letters. Some things are hard to understand, which the ignorant and unstable distort to their destruction, just as they do with the other scriptures."

After over two thousand years, a few isolated statements attributed to the Apostle Paul are often used to vilify, reject, disrespect, and deny women the opportunity to serve in the Lord's church based solely on their gender. While some believe this reflects God's will and design, others are uncertain about this interpretation. Additionally, this stance likely did not align with the views of the Apostle Paul himself. The scripture is clear: Paul did not oppose women in church leadership. He would not have had the authority to do so, even if he had wanted to. Paul was a vessel used to help establish the New Testament church and would not hold authority over all Gentile churches indefinitely.

Even during his time, Paul's influence over the church was limited and marginal. Even the Apostle Paul acknowledged that he only had the authority and impact of the churches with whom he had connections. The apostle says in 2 Corinthians 10:13-14, "We will not boast about things done outside our area of authority. We will boast only about what has happened within the boundaries of the work God has given us, which includes our working with you. We are not reaching beyond these boundaries when we claim authority over you as if we had never visited you. We were the first to travel to Corinth with the Good News of Christ."

It is essential to understand that no words spoken by the Apostle Paul should be viewed as a permanent mandate against or a limitation on women's service within the church. God has no bias and shows no favoritism; He chooses and uses whomever He wills. Christ Jesus is the head of the church, and He alone determines who serves, how they serve, and in what capacity. When God saves, gender is not a consideration. When God endows someone with His Spirit and power, gender does not matter. When God anoints, gender is not considered. When God calls, gender is irrelevant. God will use whoever is willing and available, as He looks at the heart.

It is unlikely that the words of the Apostle Paul can be considered lasting, enduring, and universally applicable across all times, cultures, and generations. No statement made by the apostle over two thousand years ago, in a society and cultural context that bears no resemblance to the present, should restrict or deny a woman's privileges, access, and opportunities today. While the Apostle Paul's words were necessary and practical for his time, it is essential to recognize that his teachings and instructions were intended to address the specific issues faced by the churches of that era.

The Apostle Paul would not recognize the present church. He could not have envisioned a society filled with highly educated, seminary-trained, gifted, and anointed scholars, theologians, teachers, preachers, evangelists, and international female missionaries. The Apostle Paul was constrained by his knowledge, experiences, and exposure to the society, culture, practices, and customs of the only world he knew. Every word he spoke was limited and influenced by his understanding and worldview of the 1st century. Paul could not envision that the world would eventually become much larger and more complex and that future societies would vastly differ from his time.

LUCY FARROW

(1851-1911)

Lucy Farrow, born into slavery in Virginia and the niece of abolitionist Frederick Douglass, was the pastor of a Holiness church in Houston, Texas, in 1905. That year, Charles Parnham from Bethel Bible College hired her as a governess for his children, leaving her church in the care of her friend William Seymour.

In 1906, William Seymour invited Lucy Farrow to Los Angeles to teach "glossolalia" to the people he prayed with for revival. Her arrival sparked what became known as the Azusa Street Revival. Through her touch, people were filled with the Holy Spirit, and her ministry demonstrated healing and the power of prayer. From Azusa Street, her influence spread throughout the Southern United States, Liberia, and West Africa.

> "I cannot be called anything other than what I am, a Christian."
>
> —**Vibia Perpetua (ca. 182-203)**

"It must not be tolerated that Christ should be unknown through our silence, and sinners unwarned through our negligence."

—Charles Spurgeon

8
WHAT DID JESUS SAY?

> **Matthew 28:8-10,** "The women sprinted from the tomb. They were terrified but filled with great joy and rushed to give the disciples the angel's message. And as they went, Jesus met them and greeted them. And they ran to him, grasped his feet, and worshiped him. Then Jesus said to them, "Don't be afraid! Go tell my brothers to leave for Galilee, and they will see me there."

In the scriptures, Jesus emphasizes that love is the most excellent quality a disciple can possess. He does not present love as a mere suggestion or option; it is essential. Love is vital for the life of anyone who follows Christ. Followers of Christ are expected to embody his character to such an extent that when the world sees us, it sees a reflection of Christ himself. Jesus stated that the world will recognize us as his followers by the love we demonstrate, particularly the love we express toward one another. So, where is our love?

As Christians, we have a responsibility to love. We are commanded to showcase God's love to the lost world and let Christ's love draw them closer to Him. This love should first be shared among fellow Christians. The work of Christian ministry can be taxing, tedious, and exhausting, to say the least. We cannot afford to be deliberately divisive among ourselves as we labor for Christ.

The Bible teaches us that the kingdom of God is one body of

many members, each of whom is invaluable. Every individual has a specific task to fulfill, regardless of gender. God is the one who assigns these tasks; He is the potter, and we are the clay. As His vessels and instruments, we are called to serve the purpose He has created us. As ministers of Jesus Christ, we each have a responsibility toward one another as brothers and sisters adopted into the family of God. Our primary obligation is to love one another.

Too often, we overlook the commandment that Jesus gave, which He said is greater than all others: "A new command I give you: Love one another. As I have loved you, so you must love one another. By this everyone will know that you are my disciples if you love one another" (John 13:34-35).

Where is our love? As ministers of Christ, we must unite with the common purpose of advancing the kingdom of God. Gender should not be an issue when the teaching, doctrine, and practices are theologically and biblically sound and when souls are consistently added to the kingdom. We must remember that God can use whomever He chooses. Both women and men can be effective in His work. No one can determine Heaven or Hell for another; that responsibility belongs to our great God. The gender of a church leader, Bishop/Pastor, Elder, Overseer, or Deacon is of little significance regarding the service of Christ. The Spirit of God can lead and direct everyone in truth.

The tricks and tactics of the evil one are both clever and subtle. The emphasis on gender serves as a tactic of division, distracting the church and preventing unity. Male and female ministers are not enemies; instead, the adversary has exploited gender-related attitudes to weaken our focus and diminish our collective strength in the fight against his kingdom. As stated in Ephesians 6:12, "We are not fighting against flesh-and-blood enemies, but against evil rulers and authorities of the unseen world, against mighty powers in this dark world, and evil spirits in the heavenly places."

As ministers of Christ, both men and women are entrusted with teaching and preaching the Gospel. But why should it matter who leads, preaches, or proclaims the good news of Jesus if the Savior is exalted above all? Jesus said, "If I am lifted, I will draw all people to myself." What truly matters is that Christ is lifted and exalted. It is of little importance who carries out this work, nor does it depend on titles or positions. If the message is effectively delivered, God is pleased.

As followers of Christ, we must strive to be more tolerant, encouraging, and supportive of God's work. We must be willing to abandon our prejudices, man-made ideas, and biased perspectives. It is time to stop justifying our ignorance and accept that God uses men and women in His vineyard. Although this may be hard to accept, God is not concerned about titles or positions; He is focused on the work of soul-winning. Jesus does not care about gender; both males and females are called to fulfill the role of evangelist.

The misguided interpretations of certain scriptures attributed to the Apostle Paul are insignificant when we consider God's undeniable anointing and transformative power in the lives and ministries of countless female pastors worldwide. God uses women as pastors, teachers, evangelists, and missionaries from diverse backgrounds and cultures to transform lives, set captives free, and win souls for His kingdom. This reality is irrefutable!

Jesus reminds us that a house divided against itself cannot stand. As Christians, we must unite to win souls for God's kingdom. We should not waste our time debating who is qualified to lead and preach the free and life-changing message of the Gospel (the Good News). God is fully capable of overseeing His Word and His church. Our thoughts and opinions do not limit Him. His anointing is boundless and unrestricted. The ways and thoughts of God are beyond our understanding. He tells us, "My thoughts are not your thoughts, neither are your ways my ways," says the LORD. "For as the heavens are higher than the earth, so are my ways higher than your ways and my thoughts than your thoughts" (Isaiah 55:8-9).

If Deborah could serve as a judge in Israel for 40 years, then women today should certainly be able to lead, preach the gospel, and hold any position equal to their male counterparts. If a woman possesses the qualifications of an excellent minister, her gender should not disqualify her from any aspect of leadership in the Lord's service. The scripture states, "As many as received him, to them He gave the power to become the sons of God, even to them that believe in his name" (John 1:12).

No woman called by God should be denied the right to minister in any capacity. Like her male counterparts, she deserves the opportunity to demonstrate her calling. Who can stop her if God genuinely calls her to serve and lead in His house? Those who attempt to hinder or prevent her will ultimately be unsuccessful.

Opposing women in ministry means not just standing against them but fighting against the mighty hand of God. When men fail to recognize and acknowledge God's hand, movement, and work, they often mislabel it as evil. It was the religious elite of Jesus' time who called the apostles' work demonic. However, we can reflect on the wise counsel of Rabbi Gamaliel in Acts 5:38-39, which states: "If their purpose or activity is of human origin, it will fail. But if it is from God, you cannot stop them; you will only find yourselves fighting against God."

If anyone believes that a woman should not serve in any area of the church, it's important to remember that God is in control. It is His church, and He has ultimate authority. In Matthew 13:27-30, Jesus says, "The farmer's workers went to him and said, 'Sir, the field where you planted that good seed is full of weeds! Where did they come from?' 'An enemy has done this!' the farmer exclaimed. 'Should we pull out the weeds?' they asked. 'No,' he replied, 'you'll uproot the wheat if you do. Let both grow together until the harvest. Then I will tell the harvesters to sort out the weeds, tie them into bundles and burn them, and put the wheat in the barn."

For this reason, the Apostle Paul reminds us in 1 Corinthians 15:58, "Dear brothers and sisters, be strong and steady, always enthusiastic about the Lord's work, for you know that nothing you do for the Lord is ever useless."

LOUISA WOOSLEY

(1862-1952)

At twelve, Louisa Woosley felt called to serve in the Lord's vineyard, recognizing the plentiful harvest and few laborers. She hoped her husband would become a preacher, but he did not share that desire. Intensifying in her calling, she studied her Bible and noted all mentions of women. By the end, she was convinced that God had important work for women, as He was impartial.

One Sunday, in the absence of a pastor, Louisa Woosley delivered her first sermon, which ignited her desire to become a minister. In 1889, the Nolin Presbytery ordained her, making her the first woman ordained in any Presbyterian denomination and the first in any Reformed tradition in America.

For the next thirty years, her ordination was a source of significant controversy within the Kentucky synod. She authored a defense of women's ordination titled "Shall Women Preach?" Her ministry was characterized by courage and determination in the face of severe discrimination.

"She was created in the image of God! How can anyone dare slander the vessel that bears such noble imprint? ... And if anyone says that it was a woman, Lady Eve, who caused man's fall from Paradise, I would say that man gained more through Mary than he lost through Eve."

-Christine de Pizan (ca. 1364-1430)

"A preacher, without boldness, is like a smooth file, a knife without an edge, a sentinel afraid to let off his gun."

—William Gurnall

9
WHAT DID JESUS DO?

> **John 4:25-27,** "The woman said, "I know the Messiah is coming—the one who is called Christ. When he comes, he will explain everything to us." Then Jesus told her, "I am the Messiah!" Just then, his disciples came back. They were shocked to find him talking to a woman, but none had the nerve to ask, "What do you want with her?" or "Why are you talking to her?"

Jesus was, above all, a revolutionary and a man ahead of his time regarding his views, practices, and actions toward women. Either Paul believed his views on women were superior to those of Jesus, or he has been wholly misunderstood. The Bible clearly states that a servant is no greater than his master; therefore, what the master does, the servant must also do. As a bondservant of the Lord Jesus Christ, Paul was obligated to follow the example of his master and adhere to His principles.

When we examine the Gospel of Luke, we find that Jesus mentioned, interacted with, or spoke positively about women on numerous occasions—specifically, over twenty-three times in scripture. Jesus accepted women and valued them for their character and qualities. As God, He looked beyond outward appearances and focused on the heart. Throughout scripture, and even today, women often demonstrate a greater willingness, availability, and unwavering commitment to serving the Lord than many of their male counterparts.

Among all the books in the Bible, Luke's Gospel is notable for its focus on God's care and interest in women. The tenderness and gentleness of women never intimidated Jesus. He often challenged the cultural biases and traditions of His time. For instance, He allowed a woman to wash His feet with her tears and dry them with her hair (Luke 7:36-50). This act demonstrated sincere repentance, and Jesus embraced it without embarrassment or disgust, regardless of the reactions from those around Him.

During a time when rabbis would openly pray, thanking God that they were born Jewish men and not Gentiles (dogs) or women, Jesus invited women and embraced them within his circle of followers and friends. Consistently, women ministered to Jesus in various and unique ways. Jesus conveyed to women that they had value, purpose, and usefulness. Jesus let them know they were intelligent and worthy of God's interest, concern, and love. Because of His unbiased love, women served him tirelessly and selflessly from his earthly ministry until his death, burial, and resurrection. According to Luke 23:27-29, the daughters of Jerusalem followed Jesus and wept for Him as they made their way down what is known as *"The Street of Sorrows."*

Jesus fully understood the social and cultural biases and prejudices against women. He was sensitive to their needs, concerns, and overall well-being. It was his desire and objective to alleviate the burdens and struggles faced by women. Unlike many other religious leaders of his time, Jesus did not impose his rights and privileges on women. Instead, he actively sought opportunities to serve them. For instance, in Luke 7:11-17, Jesus recognized that a woman could be left in poverty and desperation if she had no male benefactor or relative to support her. To help her, he raised the son of a widow from Nain back to life.

At the synagogue, Jesus healed a woman in front of a group of men, effectively challenging cultural and traditional norms. From the back, he called her to the front of the room, interrupting a sacred time of teaching the Holy Scriptures among Jewish men to minister to her. He spoke to her kindly, addressing her publicly and openly in front of the men, and he touched her—an action that a respectful and devout Jewish man or rabbi would typically avoid. This act went against Jewish laws and practices, yet Jesus affirmed her worth and value in a male-dominated society.

In Luke 13:15, Jesus challenged the men by asking, "Don't you untie your oxen and donkeys to take them to be watered on the Sabbath?" He pointed out that they secretly broke the Sabbath by doing so. Jesus further highlighted the woman's value by saying in Luke 6:16, "This woman is worth far more than any animal you have. She is not an animal; she is a daughter of Abraham." With this statement, Jesus restored her to her rightful place. He willingly risked His life for her at that moment, just as he had done previously when confronted with the woman caught in adultery, even though they hadn't brought the man involved.

By openly ministering to a woman in the synagogue, Jesus humiliated His opponents. As a result of His kindness, gentleness, and compassion, He ultimately went to the cross. Throughout all the Gospels, including Luke, there is no instance in which Jesus devalues or dismisses the worth of a woman. Are we not called to follow the example of our master, Jesus? We should emulate Him as His disciple, for a disciple is never more remarkable than the master or teacher.

We must remember the promise in Joel 2:28-29, reiterated in Acts 2:17-18. Joel 2:28-29 states, "It will come about afterward that I will pour out My Spirit on all mankind; your sons and daughters will prophesy, your old men will dream dreams, and your young men will see visions. Even on My male and female servants, I will pour out My Spirit in those days." Acts 2:17-18 reinforces this message: "'And it shall be in the last days,' God says, 'that I will pour forth of My Spirit upon all mankind; your sons and your daughters shall prophesy, your young men shall see visions, and your old men shall dream dreams. I will pour forth My Spirit even on My bondslaves, both men and women, in those days, and they shall prophesy."

AGNES WHITE DIFFEE

(1886-1970)

At the age of sixteen, Agnes White Diffee became the youngest revivalist in the country. Despite her effectiveness as an evangelist, she once expressed her reluctance to accept the call to ministry, saying, "I tried to be excused from answering the call because I was a woman. I wouldn't have minded if I had been a man, but being called a 'woman preacher' was more than I could bear."

In 1919, she was ordained as the senior pastor of a Nazarene church in Amity, Arkansas, and later went on to pastor First Nazarene in Little Rock. Over twenty years, her congregation grew from fewer than 300 members to over 1,000. Diffee served as a pastor for thirty-five years and once encouraged young women by saying, "I urge young women to keep an ear turned to Heaven for the call of God to preach the gospel."

"There needs a great deal of spiritual wisdom to cry aloud against sin without wounding the faith of God's dear children, as to their interest in Christ and his Salvation."

-Anne Dutton (ca. 1692–1765)

"Preach not calmly and quietly as though you were asleep, but preach with fire, pathos, and passion."

—Charles Spurgeon

10

JEREMIAH'S DECLARATION

> **1 Corinthians 9: 16**, "I cannot boast about preaching the Good News. God compels me to do it. How terrible for me if I didn't preach the Good News!"

Jeremiah's declaration resonates with many Christians today but was unique for his time. No other character in scripture expressed a statement quite like this man of God. His declaration stemmed from his service, reverence, and intimate relationship with God. He deeply understood God's power, mercy, compassion, desires, and heart. Jeremiah felt compelled to share everything he knew about God, which motivated his proclamation about the divine.

The Old Testament prophet Jeremiah described how the word of God burned within him, consuming him like a raging fire that was always ready to break free. He expressed his inability to contain the truth that filled his mind, heart, conscience, soul, and spirit. Jeremiah's declaration reflects the experience of many preachers today; once you come to know God intimately and personally, it becomes nearly impossible to hold back His truth. The truth of His words ignites a fire within, compelling all to share it.

Because God is so great and entirely beyond human understanding, whenever he is experienced, men and women are compelled to share His goodness and unimaginable love with others. Every faithful minister seeks to communicate God's greatness and the depth of their heartfelt connection to Him. There is no distinction between the male and female preacher; the burning within is the same.

Our relationship with God and the gift of the Holy Spirit profoundly changes our perspective. Encountering God moves us beyond conventional logic and wisdom. While the pressures, challenges, and demands of ministry can be overwhelming, the undeniable power within us and our understanding of God compels us to share His message boldly. No man or woman of God can overlook God's indescribable power and presence in their lives. As a result, they are driven to share His statutes, laws, and truths. God shows no favoritism; there is no distinction in this calling. Like the prophet Jeremiah, male and female ministers sometimes feel the overwhelming urge to stop teaching, witnessing, evangelizing, and preaching. However, regardless of gender, we cannot remain silent. We must proclaim God's truth.

When women preachers encounter challenges, ridicule, and harassment from those who should support them in achieving a common goal, many feel overwhelmed and tempted to give up. However, like the prophet Jeremiah, they experience a sense of constraint. Despite the trials, heartaches, and pains they endure—along with direct attacks and suffering—they remain devoted servants of Christ, committed to fulfilling God's work.

Women preachers, much like the prophet Jeremiah, often face both direct and indirect challenges from those who claim to possess the spirit of God, characterized by love. Unfortunately, they frequently encounter a lack of true love (agape), rejection, denial, and disrespect. Despite these obstacles, countless women preachers worldwide remain dedicated to their calling and bringing souls to God's kingdom. Many have embraced the words of the Apostle Paul in 2 Timothy 2:3-4, 10-13: "Endure suffering along with me, as a good soldier of Christ Jesus. Soldiers don't get entangled in the affairs of civilian life, for then they cannot please the officer who enlisted them... I am willing to endure anything if it will bring salvation and eternal glory in Christ Jesus to those God has chosen. This is a trustworthy saying: If we die with him, we will live with him. If we endure hardship, we will reign with him. If we deny him, he will deny us. If we are unfaithful, he remains faithful, for he cannot deny who he is."

As co-laborers, like their male counterparts, they consistently deal significant blows to the kingdom of Satan. They fight on despite facing danger, suffering, heartache, and discouragement. Despite biases, prejudice, and the perceived inconvenience of their gender, like the prophet Jeremiah, female preachers have no choice. Their hearts resonate with Jeremiah's words when he says, "Then I said, 'I will not make mention of him, nor speak any more in his name.' But his word was in my heart like a burning fire shut up in my bones..." (Jeremiah 20:9).

AIMEE SEMPLE MCPHERSON

(1890-1944)

Before turning twenty, Aimee Semple McPherson became a widow while serving as a missionary in China. After returning to America, she remarried and had two children by the age of twenty-three and was dying of pancreatic cancer. During her illness, she heard God asking, "Now, will you go?" This led her to begin her ministry as a traveling evangelist.

Settling with her in Los Angeles, Aimee McPherson established a permanent ministry. Within the first seven years, her Angelus Temple church attracted 40 million visitors.

Aimee McPherson was a prominent media figure and one of the most photographed individuals of her time. She is often regarded as the first celebrity pastor. She preached over twenty sermons each week and was the first preacher to use radio to broadcast messages. A reporter once noted her captivating ability to speak for an hour to an hour and a half without interruption, holding her audience captivated.

Inspired by her Salvation Army roots, McPherson mandated that all church members engage in charitable work. During the Great Depression, Angelus Temple fed 1.5 million people, becoming one of the most effective philanthropic organizations of the era.

When asked, "What is my task?" Aimee McPherson replied, "To get the gospel to every man, woman, boy, and girl worldwide in the shortest possible time!"

"This is my story; this is my song. Praising my Savior all the day long."

-Fanny Crosby (ca. 1820-1915)

"We are not responsible to God for the souls that are saved, but we are responsible to God for the Gospel that is preached and for how we preach it."

—**Charles Spurgeon**

11
FAITHFUL LABORERS

> **Colossians 3:23**, "Work willingly at whatever you do, as though you were working for the Lord rather than for people."

God has always been concerned about those in need. His primary focus has consistently been on the downtrodden, desperate, dejected, and hopeless. His apparent desire and plan are to provide help, comfort, and hope to struggling people. We see God's heart reflected in John 3:16: "For God so loved the world that He gave His only begotten Son, that whoever believes in Him shall not perish but have everlasting life."

As in Christ's time, many people today are lost and need divine help and deliverance. Those who do not know the Savior unknowingly walk in darkness. As a result of this void, countless men and women around the world feel desperate and hopeless. God actively seeks courageous, committed, and willing individuals to bring light to those living in darkness. He remains unchanged and relentless in His search, ready to use anyone available, regardless of gender.

When Jesus gave the "Great Commission," he did not limit this charge to a specific gender or "men only." Instead, he mandated male and female disciples, saying, "Go and make disciples of all nations, teaching them to observe everything I have commanded you." These instructions were given to all followers of Christ—everyone who professes to be a servant, loyal, faithful, and surrendered to the Lordship of Christ.

Today, the world resembles the days of Jesus—filled with wickedness. The hearts and minds of the masses are growing darker each day. More than ever, people—men, women, boys, and girls—desperately need the life-changing experience that comes from the living word of God. The scripture asks, "How will they hear without a preacher?" Unfortunately, few are willing to surrender their lives, aspirations, personal ambitions, and dreams for the Lord's service. Many are reluctant to deny themselves and their plans for the rewards of eternity.

God is always searching for those ready to put their hands on the plow and not look back. However, few are willing and committed to the task. In Matthew 9:36-38, it is stated, "The harvest is plentiful, but the laborers are few; therefore, pray to the Lord of the harvest to send out laborers into His harvest." God seeks laborers—those willing to work in this world, which is the harvest. Unlike humans, God is not concerned with gender. His primary and unchanging goal is to save the lost. He is neither chauvinistic nor egotistical; He is a sovereign and holy God.

God is faithful, kind, and generous, showing no favoritism. In the Parable of the Vineyard Workers, we are told in Matthew 20, "The Kingdom of Heaven is like a landowner who hires workers for his vineyard. He agrees to pay them a standard daily wage and sends them to work. At nine o'clock, he hires more workers, promising fair pay at the end of the day. He does this again at noon and three o'clock. At five o'clock, he finds more workers and asks why they are not working. They reply, "Because no one hired us." He tells them to join the others in his vineyard. That evening, he instructed the foreman to pay the workers. Those who had worked only one hour received a full day's wage. However, the workers hired first expected to receive more but were paid the same amount. They complained, saying it was unfair since they had worked all day in the heat. The owner replied, "I haven't been unfair!

You agreed to this wage, and I paid the last workers the same amount. Is it wrong for me to be generous?" "Those who are last will be first, and those who are first will be last."

Since immemorial, God has sought faithful and diligent laborers. Regardless of gender, we are all His vessels. He is the potter, and we are merely clay. God alone determines the shape we take. He alone has such authority. He creates all male or female vessels for His good pleasure. Some vessels are made for honor, while others are made for dishonor. Ultimately, He alone chooses how and for what purpose each will be used. God sends whomever He chooses into His harvest, whether male or female—not man.

Whether male or female, we are all laborers for the same master. In 1 Corinthians 3:7, we are reminded, "The ones who do the planting or watering aren't important; what matters is God, because He is the one who makes the seed grow. The one who plants and the one who waters work as a team with the same purpose, yet each will be rewarded individually based on their hard work. We are partners working together for God."

IDA B. ROBINSON

(1891-1946)

In 1924, while fasting and praying for ten days, Ida Robinson received a revelation from the Holy Spirit, saying, "Come out on Mount Sinai." On May 20, 1924, the State of Pennsylvania granted her a charter for the church she founded, Mount Sinai Holy Church of America Incorporated.

Ida B. Robinson was an American Holiness-Pentecostal and Charismatic denominational leader, founder, Senior Bishop, Presiding Prelate, and first President of Mount Sinai Holy Church of America Incorporated from 1924 to 1946.

Founded by an African American woman, Mount Sinai Holy Church of America is the only organization to maintain consistent female leadership from 1924 until February 2001.

"But Moses replied, "Are you jealous for my sake? I wish all the LORD's people were prophets, and the LORD would put his Spirit upon them all!"

Numbers 11:29

"You have nothing to do but to save souls; therefore, spend and be spent in this work."

—**John Wesley**

12

JOEL'S PROPHESY

> **Deuteronomy 10:17**, "The Lord your God is the God of gods and Lord of lords. He is the great, mighty, and awesome God who shows no partiality and cannot be bribed."

Many believe that the Scriptures teach against women in leadership roles and preaching. However, it is likely that the statements found in 1 Timothy 2:12 – "I do not permit a woman to teach or have authority over a man; she must be silent" – and 1 Timothy 3:1-2 – "If someone aspires to be a church leader, he desires an honorable position. Therefore, a church leader must be a man whose life is above reproach. He must be faithful to his wife, exercise self-control, live wisely, and have a good reputation. He must be hospitable and able to teach" – are often misinterpreted.

Moreover, in Titus 1:7-9, it is written, "A church leader is a manager of God's household; he must live a blameless life. He must not be arrogant or quick-tempered; he must not be a heavy drinker, violent, or dishonest with money. Rather, he must be hospitable and love what is good. He must live wisely and justly and lead a devout and disciplined life. He must strongly believe in the trustworthy message he was taught so that he can encourage others with wholesome teaching and refute those who oppose it."

Additionally, Titus 2:3-5 instructs older women to teach younger women and others. These passages attributed to the Apostle Paul can often be misinterpreted and misunderstood.

Although some statements may seem to limit women's roles as leaders and preachers in the Lord's house, this perspective is widely challenged and contested within the church and various denominations. Women have been involved in all aspects of ministry since the very beginning. For instance, a woman was the first to witness the risen Savior and proclaim the good news to her male counterparts. Furthermore, many women in the first century served as preachers, teachers, and leaders of house churches long before the establishment of organized religion, traditions, polity, and denominations.

The belief that women cannot fulfill roles equal to their male counterparts is challenged by the fact that this issue is raised and marginally supported by only a few phrases supposedly attributed to the Apostle Paul. Each alleged statement and phrase can be better understood considering the time's historical, situational, contextual, and cultural circumstances. Furthermore, no other writer or apostle similarly addressed or discussed women's roles or functions in the church or the Lord's service. The Apostle Paul stands alone in this commentary. Upon closer examination, it becomes clear and irrefutable that his letters were written to address specific, sensitive issues or concerns relevant to individual churches at that time.

The words of the Apostle Paul were not meant to serve as strict mandates or lasting restrictions, and they shouldn't be interpreted that way. Paul did not have insight into the future, the gospel message's widespread impact, the Church's evolution, or the development of future societies in a much larger world. He could not have conceived that the world would grow to be so much larger than anything he had known or could imagine. Paul would likely not recognize our modern society, which provides access to high-level education for both men and women and unprecedented access to information, equal rights, privileges, and opportunities for all.

Even if these words are attributed to Paul, he addressed people and churches from a completely different time, culture, and era, with social practices, traditions, and norms unfamiliar and dissimilar to today's social practices. Paul was not speaking perpetually; he was addressing the specific situations of his context.

It is unreasonable to conclude that the apostle's words bar women from preaching or church leadership. At no time was Paul given or afforded such authority. God is unconcerned with gender, titles, or positions. He cares only about accomplished work, which he calls His servants to do. The servant is not particularly important, male or female. The apostle helps us better understand this by the words recorded in 1 Corinthians 3: 4-9, "When one of you says, "I am a follower of Paul," and another says, "I follow Apollos," aren't you acting just like people of the world? After all, who is Apollos? Who is Paul? We are only God's servants through whom you believed the Good News. Each of us did the work the Lord gave us. I planted the seed in your hearts, and Apollos watered it, but God made it grow. It's not important who does the planting or who does the watering. What's important is that God makes the seed grow. The ones who plant and water work together with the same purpose. And both will be rewarded for their hard work. For we are both God's workers."

Women preachers and leaders are valuable workers of God, just like Paul and Apollos. God shows no favoritism and will use anyone eager to serve Him. It is misguided to believe that God does not call women to be preachers and leaders, even within the Church. This notion is simply untrue. Scripture provides numerous examples of women God has used as He deemed fit.

In the Old Testament, the first female preacher and leader we encounter is the Prophetess Deborah, a highly respected woman known for her wisdom and authority. Her preaching and guidance were crucial in leading Israel to victory over its enemies. Other notable female preachers include Miriam, Huldah, Anna, and Priscilla.

Traditionally, leadership has often been assumed to be a male role; however, this has not always been the case. Throughout various societies and cultures, women have held roles of authority and leadership equal to those of their male counterparts.

God uses those He chooses. The time's traditions, customs, and social norms were limiting factors in the context of the Apostle Paul. However, as the Lord of the past, present, and future, God communicated something extraordinary through the prophet Joel. Eight hundred years before the day of Pentecost, Joel spoke of God's plans by the power of the Holy Spirit. In Joel 2:28-29, the Lord said, "I will pour out my Spirit upon all people. Your sons and daughters will prophesy; your old men will dream dreams, and your young men will see visions. In those days, I will pour out my Spirit even on servants—men and women alike." Speaking of the last days, although inconceivable, God promised to give His Spirit to men and women generously. Unlike in times past, God promised to do something new, previously unknown, unrecognized, or unconsidered.

Significant miracles occurred on the day of Pentecost. Unlike in the past, when God poured His Spirit only on a select few, both Jews and non-Jews now experienced this outpouring, marking a profound shift. Previously, the Holy Spirit empowered designated individuals for specific tasks only for a limited time. However, during this event, many received the indwelling presence of the Spirit.

The Apostle Peter addressed the misinterpretations of this event in Acts 2:17-18, stating, "This is what was spoken by the prophet Joel: "In the last days, God says, I will pour out my Spirit on all people. Your sons and daughters will prophesy, your young men will see visions, and your old men will dream dreams. Even on my servants, both men and women, I will pour out my Spirit in those days, and they will prophesy."

God shows no favoritism; He loves everyone equally. He desires all people to come to a saving knowledge and faith in Christ Jesus. He is not concerned with whether the person leading, winning souls, or proclaiming the liberating and transformative message of the kingdom of God is male or female. The prophet Joel revealed that God plans to extend His gift to everyone, regardless of their background, culture, ethnicity, or gender. This is supported in Acts 10:44-45, "Even as Peter was saying these things, the Holy Spirit fell upon all who were listening to the message. The Jewish believers who came with Peter were amazed that the gift of the Holy Spirit had been poured out on the Gentiles, too."

We are in the last days, and God is doing something new. He is using both men and women to achieve His plans and objectives for His church. God does not oppose women in ministry; He has endowed them equally with the same gifts as their male counterparts for the work He calls them to. He qualifies and equips those He has chosen.

You may believe what you will, but the truth is undeniable. The proof that God has poured His Spirit on women just as He has on men is evident in the success, effectiveness, and fruit of countless ministries founded, facilitated, and led by women despite facing opposition. Although this may not align with traditional models or ideals, God uses whatever means necessary to accomplish His purposes.

We must humbly acknowledge that none of us truly understands God's mind. His thoughts and ways are different from and higher than our own. The Scriptures provide clear examples of God acting according to His will, even when it contradicts logic, reason, or human understanding. In Numbers 22, God uses a donkey to fulfill His purpose.

According to Numbers 22:28, "The Lord gave the donkey the ability to speak." The donkey was allowed to challenge his master Balaam's actions, asking, "What have I done to you that deserves you beating me three times?" If God could use a beast of burden, nothing impedes His ability to use a woman in any manner He chooses.

The idea and embrace of women in perceived nontraditional roles are a lasting and enduring challenge for many, particularly the unyielding, close-minded, and spiritually arrogant. God has the right and privilege to act as He wishes in every context, including the church. The leadership role has traditionally been reserved for men, with the expectation that they would pursue and hold these positions. However, fewer men are willing to serve in leadership roles across various contexts, including the church. An example of this can be found in the story of Deborah and General Barak. The Scriptures indicate that although Barak was expected to lead the Lord's army, he refused. Instead, he chose to depend on and trust the strength and wisdom of Deborah, a prophetess.

The traditional leadership model has predominantly featured men. However, that is not the complete picture. Throughout history, God has also used women as leaders. The Scriptures illustrate this, particularly in the story of Deborah and Barak. In Judges 4:6-9, we read:

"One day, Deborah sent for Barak son of Abinoam, who lived in Kedesh in Naphtali. She told him, 'This is what the Lord, the God of Israel, commands you: Call out 10,000 warriors from the tribes of Naphtali and Zebulun at Mount Tabor. I will call out Sisera, the commander of Jabin's army, along with his chariots and warriors, to the Kishon River. I will give you victory over him.' Barak replied, 'I will go, but only if you go with me.' "Very well," she answered, "I will go with you. But you will receive no honor in this venture, for the Lord's victory over Sisera will be at the hands of a woman." This passage highlights

Barak's willingness to recognize and support Deborah's leadership, underscoring the vital role that women can play in leadership positions.

Women in church leadership is not a new concept. Several women held leadership positions in the early church and beyond. The belief that women should not or cannot be leaders is a relatively modern invention. It's important to note that the term "pastor" appears only once in Scripture, specifically in Ephesians 4:11. Even in this context, the term is less about formal license, ordination, or consecration and more about the heart and willingness to meet, attend to, and care for the spiritual and practical needs of those within their congregation.

Women have always played a crucial and significant role in the church. They have never been considered secondary to their male counterparts when they possess the same capabilities. In the New Testament church, neither men nor women were called pastors. However, both fulfilled pastoral functions, such as teaching, preaching, instructing, and caring for the spiritual and practical needs of others. Notably, no less than seven of the ten women mentioned in the Apostle Paul's writings are recognized for their associations with ministry roles. In Romans 16:1-6, the apostle identifies several women: Phoebe, Prisca, Mary, Junia, Tryphena, Tryphosa, and Persis.

There is a strong and compelling case for both male and female leaders and pastors in the Lord's church. The opposition from egotistical, arrogant, and chauvinistic men, as well as some misguided women, will not change or hinder the work and plan of the one who calls and chooses all. God can and will use whomever He desires.

Despite misinterpretations of certain statements attributed to the Apostle Paul, God will continue to empower women in ministry and church leadership. We must not overlook the authentic words and affirmation of the apostle in Galatians 3:28, which says, "There is no longer Jew or Gentile, slave or free, male and female. You are all one in Christ Jesus. And now that you belong to Christ, you are the true children of Abraham. You are his heirs, and God's promise to Abraham belongs to you."

Regardless of differing opinions about female leadership in the church, it is essential to recognize that these views are human inventions and not rooted in God's intentions. God does not favor one gender over another in leadership roles; instead, He calls us all to bear fruit and fulfill our assigned work. Clear evidence shows that God is moving in a new direction. He has answered the prayers of the faithful, and as the harvest remains plentiful while laborers are few, He is sending women to serve as laborers in His mission field.

God has kept His promise and His word. The presence of women preachers, teachers, pastors, and leaders fulfills the prophecy found in Joel 2:28-29, which states, "I will pour out my Spirit on all people. Your sons and daughters will prophesy, your old men will dream dreams, and your young men will see visions. Even on my servants, both men and women, I will pour out my Spirit in those days."

MARY J. SMALL

(1850–1945)

Although she initially opposed the idea of women preachers, Mary Smalls was licensed on January 21, 1892. Later, on January 19, 1895, she was ordained as a deacon. She worked tirelessly alongside her husband in the African Methodist Zion Church until his death and was highly revered for her contributions.

After passing her examinations, Reverend Mary Smalls became the first woman ordained as an elder. Her nomination received approval on May 23, 1898, during the Philadelphia and Baltimore connections of the Church.

The African Methodist Episcopal (A.M.E.Z.) Zion Church was the first to open high-level positions to women. As an elder, Reverend Mary J. Smalls enjoyed equal rights with any other minister, including authority over male and female church members.

"Do I think women can do this? Yes."

-Bishop Vashti Murphy McKenzie (ca. 1947-)

TO THE ELECT WOMEN IN CHRIST

Ministry work can be challenging, tiring, and often exhausting; it is not for the faint-hearted. However, God calls those He chooses. Since He shows no favoritism, female laborers are equally welcome as His servants. Just as God desires to save everyone, He invites anyone willing and available, with the right motives and heart, to serve Him as He sees fit.

Despite encountering challenges, obstacles, and rejection, stay focused and committed to the work God has called you to do. Remain faithful, loyal, and uncompromised in your ministry. Regardless of whether you are invited, welcomed, or respected, preach the Word of God, serve in leadership, seize every opportunity that God provides, and showcase your calling, anointing, and gifts.

It is not a mistake or coincidence that God has called you to this challenging, frustrating, and demanding work. God looks at the heart, unlike people who judge based on outer appearances. He seeks those who are faithful, committed, and diligent. Whether male or female, He desires those who love Him, His people, and His church—those who long to see men and women come out of darkness and into the marvelous light of Christ Jesus.

No matter what obstacles you face, keep pressing on. Never retreat or surrender. The hardships, suffering, and challenges of your ministry are worthwhile. An award awaits you and all those who have sacrificed to make soul-winning, preaching, and disciple-making their focus and priority. Only what is done for Christ endures. Serving in ministry carries eternal value; nothing is done in vain. Stay faithful amid rejection, denial, abandonment, and betrayal. Preach the gospel continually. Share the good news of Christ whenever and wherever God presents an opportunity.

As a woman of God, gifted for His service, take comfort in knowing that you, like many others, are called to a significant and holy mission. While many are called, few are chosen, and it is a privilege to be called by God. If you have counted the cost and decided to preach the kingdom of God, even in peril or death, you have genuinely been chosen. Choosing to endure ridicule, slander, and rejection may seem unreasonable and illogical to many. However, it is your only response when the Holy Spirit inspires, empowers, and compels you.

God calls both men and women into His service without preference. He looks at the heart of everyone. The world needs committed, bold, and courageous people to share the life-transforming Word of God. Many individuals are suffering, feeling oppressed, and experiencing depression and hopelessness. You can be the answer to their liberation; you hold the key to their freedom. Regardless of gender, you must preach the redemptive message of the cross of Calvary. God has called you to set the captives free. You hold the answer and must fulfill the calling in your life. Preach the word of God without apology. Take your place among God's kings and priests. Stand up and claim your position in God's holy nation.

"An infinite God can give all of Himself to each of His children. He does not distribute Himself that each may have a part, but to each one, He gives all of Himself as fully as if there were no others."

—AW Tozer

TO MALE LEADERS

As emissaries of the Lord Jesus, we have been called to a sacred duty and entrusted with the holy word of our great God. We have been chosen to be leaders, teachers, proclaimers, and stewards of the truth. Considering this calling, we are responsible for preaching and being faithful students and diligent scholars of God's word. We are held to the same charge the apostle gave his young protege in 2 Timothy 2:15: "Work hard so you can present yourself to God and receive His approval. Be a good worker who does not need to be ashamed and correctly explains the word of truth."

As leaders in the Lord's church, we have both an opportunity and a responsibility to ensure that ministry work to advance God's kingdom is carried out effectively and without obstacles. Regardless of our personal opinions, biases, or prejudices, we have an obligation—and a privilege—to support, rather than hinder, the efforts of our female counterparts in the Gospel. God shows no partiality; He has called both men and women to the work of the "Great Commission." We should strive to be supporters, not obstacles, to the ministry and work of our fellow laborers, regardless of gender, as this pleases God.

For too long, we have remained silent and passive, allowing the unchallenged teachings of our leadership, along with the practices of our churches and denominations, to shape our views on women in ministry. This has led to unnecessary and unjust disrespect, rejection, denial, and criticism directed at many of our female colleagues. This must come to an end. We need to be bold, daring, and courageous. We must be willing to take a stand to support our sisters in ministry. Who are we to deny, hinder, or impede their right, access, and opportunity to serve in ministry and contribute to advancing the kingdom of God? God favors us all equally. He anoints and gifts individuals as He sees fit, and gender does not influence His decisions.

We cannot overlook the power and anointing that is evident in the lives and ministries of countless women. It is misleading to suggest that God does not use women in equal and parallel roles in ministry alongside men. Women have demonstrated that they are equally gifted, skilled, and capable as their male counterparts in all areas of ministry. The rationale for restricting their efforts and denying them support based on their gender is both irrational and unfounded.

As men who grapple with long-standing and unexamined beliefs about women in ministry, we should take to heart the words of the Apostle Paul in Galatians 3:27-29: "You are all children of God through faith in Christ Jesus. And all who have been united with Christ in baptism have put on Christ, like putting on new clothes. There is no longer Jew or Gentile, slave or free, male or female, for you are all one in Christ Jesus. Now that you belong to Christ, you are the true children of Abraham. You are his heirs, and God's promise to Abraham belongs to you."

What benefit exists in preventing a woman from preaching and proclaiming the gospel? God does not show favoritism. His only desire is that the message of Christ be shared. He wants none to perish and for everyone to repent of their sins. Should we believe that God cares who delivers this saving message? In Luke 14:23, He instructs His disciples, "Go out into the highways and hedges, and compel them to come in, that my house may be filled." Should only men be allowed the privilege of fulfilling this mission? I think not. In fact, according to scripture, even before Mary proclaimed the risen Savior, the first preacher recorded in the Bible was a woman. Exodus 15:20-21 states, "Then Miriam the prophetess, Aaron's sister, took a tambourine in her hand, and all the women followed her, with tambourines and dancing. Miriam sang to them: 'Sing to the Lord, for He is highly exalted. The horse and its rider, He has hurled into the sea."

God's ways are beyond our understanding, and He acts according to His will. If God allowed a donkey to speak to save Balaam's life, surely He could use women to preach to save lost and dying men and women. So why is there so much concern about how He achieves that objective?

Jesus emphasized in Matthew 9:37, "The harvest is truly plentiful, but the laborers are few. Therefore, pray to the Lord of the harvest to send laborers into His harvest." Women preachers, prophetesses, teachers, evangelists, deacons, elders, and pastors are God's answer to these prayers. They should not be hindered!

Historically, women have demonstrated discipline, faithfulness, commitment, and courage. They have consistently made themselves available and willing to serve Christ, even when men have faltered, paralyzed by fear and intimidation. After the resurrection, Christ first charged women with telling his disciples, saying, "Go tell my brothers to leave for Galilee; they will see me there." Are we wiser than God?

Our primary focus and concern should be sharing God's life-changing message with as many people as possible. The gender of the messenger is not necessary; what matters is that God's unchanging desire is for the lost to hear the redeeming message of Christ. The scriptures instruct us to worship the Lord in spirit and truth, and the message of Christ embodies that truth.

Our commitment to preaching the gospel comes from a sincere heart and the undeniable truth about Jesus Christ. We should support those who are physically weaker and uplift our female counterparts who are dedicated to sharing Christ's message, winning souls, and advancing the kingdom of God.

Women are equally recipients of the Holy Spirit and active participants in fellowship with Christ. When women open their hearts and make themselves available, God will continue to use them for His purposes. We need to support and encourage them in their service to the Lord. We should not view female involvement or participation as threatening our work or ministry. The harvest is great, but the laborers are few; we all have our roles to play. As men and faithful stewards of God's word, we should remember the words in John 1:12: "But as many as received Him, to them He gave the power to become the sons of God, even to those who believe in His name."

FINAL THOUGHTS AND A PRAYER

In a world filled with depravity and desperation, where many have lost hope, it is time for the brave, courageous, and committed individuals to stand up and proclaim the enduring and unchanging truth. The world desperately needs God's life-changing and transformative Word more than ever. However, people cannot hear this truth unless there are preachers. We need willing, committed, and fearless individuals to share the saving message of Jesus Christ, our Lord.

The only way for those spiritually dead and in darkness to come into the light is by hearing the truth of Christ. The Gospel serves as the solution for morally lost and spiritually empty people. In Christ alone, the lost find peace, restoration, and redemption—there is no other way. Jesus proclaimed, "Come to me, and I will give you rest." In Christ, the desperate, the lost, and the hopeless can discover joy. However, they can only learn of this hope in Christ if there is a preacher. There must be someone—male or female—who is called, chosen, and empowered to bring light into every space of darkness. Without bias or prejudice, Christ commanded His disciples to "Go" and make disciples of all nations.

Jesus said, "I am the way, the truth, and the life," indicating that He alone is the path to life and the door to salvation. He is the only source of hope and reconciliation with God. No one can come to the

Father except through Him. However, how will people know this unless someone shares the message with them?

God has called men and women to serve and labor in His vineyard. We must learn to embrace and support each other's work, even when we may not fully understand God's purpose and will. His thoughts, plans, and ways are significantly higher than our own. It is important to remember that God can guard His word and His church, and He chooses whom He wishes to serve Him with a sincere heart, regardless of gender.

Romans 10:12 reminds us that there is no distinction between Jews and Greeks; the same Lord is Lord of all, generously granting His blessings to everyone who calls on Him. Everyone who calls on the name of the Lord will be saved.

MY PRAYER

I earnestly pray that all who have been called into the Lord's service, regardless of gender, prejudice, and bias, stand up and be counted among the brave, diligent, and undeterred Soldiers in Christ's Army. I pray that the myriad male laborers learn and discover the futility of opposing and fighting against their sisters in the faith and co-laborers and commit to holding up their hands and supporting their work and efforts to do their part to win souls for the Lord's kingdom.

I pray that God would dismantle the walls of division, creating opportunities for unity and cohesion among us. I ask that we all adopt the mind of Christ and strive to become more like Him. May we cultivate humility, patience, and tolerance for each other, being slow to speak and eager to understand God's plans, purposes, and will through the work of all faithful ministers, regardless of gender. Let us recognize that God is unbiased and welcomes everyone to serve and worship Him in spirit and truth.

I pray that we all understand that God has not called us to oversee or control the work of ministry. On the contrary, He has called us to unity and love—authentic (agape), unconditional love, especially for all the saints, remembering that those who do not have the Spirit of Christ living in them do not belong to him at all.

WOMEN MINISTRY LEADER FIRSTS

19th century

- **1815**: In 815, Clarissa Danforth was ordained in New England, becoming the first woman ordained by the Free Will Baptist denomination.

- **1853**: In 1853, Antoinette Brown Blackwell became the first woman ordained a minister in the United States. She was ordained by a church affiliated with the Congregationalist Church; however, the denomination did not recognize her ordination. Eventually, she left the church and became a Unitarian. The Congregationalists later merged with other denominations to form the United Church of Christ, which ordains women.

- **1861**: In 1861, Mary A. Will was the first woman ordained in the Wesleyan Methodist Connection by the Illinois Conference in the United States. The Wesleyan Methodist Connection later became known as the Wesleyan Church.

- **1863**: In 1863, Olympia Brown became the first woman ordained by the Universalist denomination. In 1961, the Universalists and Unitarians merged to form the Unitarian Universalist Association (UUA). This association became the first sizeable religious denomination with the most female ministers.

- **1865**: The Salvation Army was founded in 1865. Following the English Methodist tradition, both men and women were ordained. However, Eleanor M. Davison is believed to have been the first woman ordained in the Methodist tradition, which occurred in 1866.

- **1880**: 1880 Anna Howard Shaw became the first woman ordained in the Methodist Protestant Church, an American denomination that later merged with others to form the United Methodist Church.

- **1883**: 1883 Ellen G. White was the first woman ordained in the Seventh-day Adventist Church by the Michigan Conference in the United States. She was also one of the founders of the Seventh-day Adventist denomination.

- **1888**: 1888 Fidelia Gillette may have been the first ordained woman in Canada. She served the Universalist congregation in Bloomfield, Ontario, between 1888 and 1889 and was presumably ordained in 1888 or earlier.

- **1889**: In 1889, the Nolin Presbytery of the Cumberland Presbyterian Church ordained Louisa Woosley as the first female minister of the Cumberland Presbyterian Church in the USA.

- **1889**: In 1889, Ella Niswonger became the first woman ordained in the American United Brethren Church, which later merged with other denominations to form the American United Methodist Church.

- **1890**: 1890 Mary Sterling became the first woman ordained as a minister by the German Baptist Brethren Church in America.

- **1892**: In 1892, Anna Hanscombe was believed to be the first woman ordained by the parent bodies, who later formed the Church of the Nazarene in 1919.

- **1894**: 1894 Julia A.J. Foote was the first woman ordained in the African Methodist Episcopal Zion Church.

Early 20th century

- **1911**: In 1911, Anna Allebach was the first Mennonite woman to be ordained.
- **1911**: 1911 Anne Zernike was ordained as a church minister by the Mennonite Church in the Netherlands, becoming the first female minister in the Netherlands and Europe.
- **1912**: In 1912, Olive Winchester, born in America, became the first woman ordained by a trinitarian Christian denomination in the United Kingdom when the Church of the Nazarene ordained her.
- **1914**: The Assemblies of God was founded in 1914, and its first women pastors were ordained.
- **1917**: In 1917, the Congregationalist Church (England and Wales) ordained its first woman, Constance Coltman (née Todd), at the King's Weigh House in London.
- **1918**: 1918 Alma Bridwell White became the first woman ordained bishop in the United States. Rosa Gutknecht and Elise Pfister were the first women in Switzerland to be ordained as pastors.

1920's

- **1920**: 1920 Riek Rappold became the first woman ordained by the Remonstrant Church in the Netherlands.
- **1922**: In 1922, the Central Conference of American Rabbis in the Jewish Reform movement stated that "...woman cannot justly be denied the privilege of ordination." However, the first

woman to be ordained in Reform Judaism, Sally Priesand, was not ordained until 1972.

- **1927:** Winifred Kiek was the first woman ordained in the Christian ministry in Australia on June 13, 1927, in South Australia with the Congregational Union of Australia (now part of the Uniting Church in Australia).
- **1929:** Maria Izabela Wiłucka-Kowalska became the first woman ordained by the Old Catholic Mariavite Church in Poland. Jantine Haumersen was the first woman ordained pastor by the Evangelical Lutheran Church in the Netherlands.

1930's

- **1930:** The Presbyterian Church in the United States of America ordained its first woman elder, Sarah E. Dickson.
- **1935:** Rabbi Regina Jonas became the first woman to be ordained as a rabbi after being privately ordained by a German rabbi.

1940's

- **1940:** Maren Sørensen became the first woman ordained in Denmark.
- **1943:** Ilse Härter and Hannelotte Reiffen were ordained in the German Confessing Church (Bekennende Kirche) on January 12, 1943.
- **1944:** Florence Li Tim Oi became the first woman ordained as an Anglican priest.
- **1947:** The Lutheran Protestant Church began ordaining women as priests, as did the Czechoslovak Hussite Church.

- **1948:** The Evangelical Lutheran Church of Denmark and the African Methodist Episcopal Church started to ordain women.
- **1949:** The Old Catholic Church (in the U.S.) began ordaining women. Élisabeth Schmidt became the first woman ordained pastor of the Reformed Church of France.

1950's

- **1954:** Bé Ruys became the first woman ordained as a Dutch Reformed minister by the Dutch Ecumenical Congregation in Berlin, Germany.
- **1956:** The Presbyterian Church in the United States of America ordained its first female minister, Margaret Towner.
- **1957:** Mary Matz became the first female minister ordained within the Moravian Church.
- **1958:** Women ministers in the Church of the Brethren were given full ordination with the same status as men.
- **1959**: Ietske Jansen became the first woman ordained as a minister by the Dutch Reformed Church in the Netherlands.

1960s

- **1960:** The Church of Sweden began ordaining women as priests. Elisabeth Djurle, Ingrid Persson, and Margit Sahlin were the first women to be ordained.
- 1961: Ingrid Bjerkås became the first woman to be ordained as a minister of the Church of Norway.
- **1964:** Addie Elizabeth Davis became the first Southern Baptist woman ordained. However, the Southern Baptist Convention ended the practice of ordaining women in 2000, although existing female pastors are allowed to continue their roles.

- **1965:** Rachel Henderlite became the first woman ordained in the Presbyterian Church in the United States, ordained by the Hanover Presbytery in Virginia.

- **1969:** Catherine McConnachie was ordained as the first woman minister in the Church of Scotland by the Presbytery of Aberdeen and served as assistant minister at St George's Tillydrone in Aberdeen.

1970s

- **1970:** On November 22, Elizabeth Alvina Platz became the first woman ordained by the Lutheran Church in America, making her the first woman ordained by any Lutheran denomination in the U.S. Barbara Andrews became the first woman ordained by the American Lutheran Church in December 1970. Joyce Bennett and Jane Hwang were the first regularly ordained priests in the Anglican Church in Hong Kong.

- **1972:** Freda Smith became the first female minister to be ordained by the Metropolitan Community Church. Following Regina Jonas, a rabbinical seminary ordained Sally Priesand as America's first female rabbi.

- **1973:** Emma Sommers Richards became the first Mennonite woman ordained as a pastor of a Mennonite congregation (Lombard Mennonite Church in Illinois).

- **1974:** Sandy Eisenberg Sasso was the first female rabbi ordained in Reconstructionist Judaism.

- **1974:** Auður Eir Vilhjálmsdóttir became the first woman ordained in the Evangelical Lutheran Church of Iceland.

- **1975:** Dorothea W. Harvey became the first woman ordained by the Swedenborgian Church.

1990's

- **1992:** In 1992, Naamah Kelman, born in the United States, became the first female rabbi ordained in Israel.
- **1993:** From 1993 to 2006, Rosemarie Kohn was bishop of the Hamar diocese. She was Norway's and the Nordic countries' first female bishop.
- **1994:** In 1994, Lia Bass was ordained by the Jewish Theological Seminary in New York, thus becoming the first Latin-American female rabbi in the world and the first woman from Brazil to be ordained as a rabbi.
- **1995:** In May 1995, Bola Odeleke became the first woman to be ordained a bishop in Africa, specifically Nigeria.
- **1996:** On December 21, 1996, Gloria Shipp of the Gamilaroi nation became the first Aboriginal woman ordained priest in the Anglican Church of Australia, in the Diocese of Bathurst.
- **1997:** In 1997, Chava Koster, born in the Netherlands and ordained in the United States, became the first female rabbi from the Netherlands.
- **1999:** In 1999, the Independent Presbyterian Church of Brazil permitted the ordination of women as clergy or elders.

21st century

- **2000:** The African Methodist Episcopal Church has elected and consecrated Vashti Murphy McKenzie as its first female bishop.
- **2001:** Eveline Goodman-Thau became the first female rabbi in Austria. She was born in Austria but ordained in Jerusalem.
- **2006:** Susan Wehle was ordained as the first American female cantor in Jewish Renewal in 2006; however, she died in 2009.

- **2007:** Kay Goldsworthy became the first woman to be consecrated as a bishop in the Anglican Church of Australia at St George's Cathedral, Perth, on 22 May 2008.
- **2009:** Alysa Stanton was ordained at a Reform Jewish seminary in Cincinnati and became the world's first Black female rabbi.

2010's

- **2010:** Alina Treiger became the first female rabbi to be ordained in Germany since World War II (the very first female rabbi ordained in Germany was Regina Jonas, ordained in 1935).
- **2011:** Sandra Kviat became the first woman from Denmark to be a rabbi, ordained in England.
- The American Catholic Church in the United States, ACCUS, ordained their first woman priest, Kathleen Maria MacPherson, on June 12, 2011.
- **2012:** Jo Henderson became the first Anglican priest ordained in the United Arab Emirates.
- **2013:** Mimi Kanku Mukendi became the first female pastor ordained by the Communauté Evangélique Mennonite au Congo (Mennonite Evangelical Community of Congo), although they voted to ordain women as pastors in 1993.
- **2014:** Fanny Sohet Belanger was ordained in America, becoming the first French female priest in the Episcopal Church.
- **2014:** The Lutheran Church in Chile ordained Rev. Hanna Schramm, born in Germany, as its first female pastor.
- **2015:** Mira Rivera became the first Filipino American woman to be ordained as a rabbi.
- **2015:** In 2015, Libby Lane became the first woman ordained as a bishop in the Church of England. She was the first woman appointed as a bishop by this church.

- **2018:** 2018 Denise Donato was ordained as the first female bishop in the Ecumenical Catholic Communion.

2020's

- **2020:** The Anglican Diocese of Cape Coast ordained its first female priest, Vida Gyabeng Frimpong.
- **2022:** The Evangelical Church of the Augsburg Confession in Poland officially ordained women as pastors for the first time.
- **2023:** On January 22, 2023, Sally Azar was ordained by the Evangelical Lutheran Church in Jordan and the Holy Land during a ceremony held at the Church of the Redeemer in Jerusalem. This historic event made her the first female Palestinian pastor in the Holy Land.
- **2024:** The Lutheran Church of Australia's Synod approved the ordination of women as pastors.

www.ingramcontent.com/pod-product-compliance
Lightning Source LLC
Chambersburg PA
CBHW062114080426
42734CB00012B/2855